SUFI WISDOM

SUNY Series in Islam
Edited by Seyyed Hossein Nasr

SUFI WISDOM

Marietta T. Stepaniants

STATE UNIVERSITY OF NEW YORK PRESS

Published by
State University of New York Press, Albany

Printed in the United States of America

For information, address State University of New York Press,
State University Plaza, Albany, N.Y., 12246

Production by Cathleen Collins
Marketing by Nancy Farrell

Library of Congress Cataloging in Publication Data

Stepaniants, M. T. (Marietta Tigranovna)
Sufi wisdom / Marietta T. Stepaniants.
p. cm. — (SUNY Series in Islam)
Rev. ed. of: Filosofskie aspekty sufizma.
Includes bibliographical references (p.) and index.
ISBN 0-7914-1795-6 (alk. paper). — ISBN 0-7914-1796-4 (pbk. : alk. paper)
1. Sufism—Doctrines. I. Stepaniants, M. T. (Marietta Tigranovna) Filosofskie aspekty sufizma. II. Title. III. Series.
BP189.3.S7413 1994
297'.4—dc20 93-545
CIP

10 9 8 7 6 5 4 3 2 1

Contents

Introduction

The interest in Sufism in Russia was originally determined by purely pragmatic considerations of a political nature. The tsarist authorities, concerned with the activities of the Sufi orders in the Muslim-populated areas, regarded them with suspicion. It is worth noting that one of the first books on Sufism in Russia was *The Book of Systems or the State of the Muslim Religion* by D. Kantemir, published at the personal order of Tsar Peter the Great.

The acitive role played by the Sufi movement, particularly the murids in the Caucasus and the ishans in Central Asia, was regarded as anti-Russian. The Sufis were accused of "stirring up and fanning enmity and hatred for Russians."[1] A particularly hostile tone was typical of Christian missionaries.

Academic research on Sufism started in Russia at the turn of the twentieth century. The study of Persian poetry greatly stimulated interest in Islamic mysticism (this was how V. Zhukovsky and A. Krimsky became involved in the subject).

Zhukovsky's writings focus primarily on early Persian Sufis. Worth mentioning here are his *Man and Cognition in the Views of the Persian Mysitcs* (1895); *The Songs of Hermit from Herat* (1895); and *The Mysteries of the Union with God in Deeds of Hermit Abu Said* (1899), dedicated to one of the founders of the oriental school of Sufism, Abū Saʿīd b. Abū 'l-Khayr (967–1049). Zhukovsky also prepared for publication *The kasf al-Muhjub* by al Ḥudjwīrī (d. ca. 1077), which appeared posthumously in 1926.

The main writings by Krimsky are *Essay on the Development of Taṣawwuf till the 3rd Century of Hijra* (1896); an article on Sufism in the famous *Encyclopedia Dictionary* edited by F. A. Brokhaus and I. A. Efron (1901); and *History of Persia, Its Literature and Dervish Theosophy* (1914–17). Krimsky considered Sufism to be pantheistic theosophy with the "pronounced deism of Islam" (*Istoriya Persii. . .Chast II*, p. 39). He was of the opinion that *taṣawwuf* and dervishism, though persecuted by "orthodox Muslim clergy," nevertheless succeeded in maintaining "a great influence on the common people in Persia, while for the educated people it was a practical free-thinking philosophy" (ibid., p. 94).

Among a few Russian prerevolutionary scholars who were engaged in Sufi studies the name of A. Shmidt must certainly be mentioned. He dedicated his M.A. thesis (1914) to an Egyptian sufi, ʿAbd al-Wahhāb ash-Sha'rani (1493–1565). Shmidt, like Krimsky, emphasized the antiorthodox orientation of *tasawwuf.* The great accomplishment of this scholar was the publication of ash-Sha'rani's *Scattered Pearls*.

Sufi ideas found reception among Russian philosophers prone to the mystic perception of the world. Noteworthy in this respect is Semyon Ludvigovich Frank,[2] who defined his views as Christian realism. In the introduction to *The Unknowable: An Ontological Introduction to the Philosophy of Religion*, which summed up "the last results" of his thought presented in their "systemic unity," Frank acknowledged as "the foundation" of his philosophy the *philosophia perenis* of Platonism and in particular of Neo-Platonism and Christian Platonism penetrating the whole history of European philosophy starting from Plotinus, Dionysius the Pseudo-Areopagite, and St. Augustine up to Baader and Vladimir Solovyov. This philosophy in principle coincided with speculative mysticism (S. L. Frank, *Sochineniya*, p. 183). Frank pointed out that he preferred not to quote the opinions of others. However, there are some revealing epigraphs in the above-mentioned book. The first, prefacing the book as a whole, is from Nicolas of Cusa (whom Frank considered to be his "only teacher"): "Attingitur inattingibile inattingibilliter" ("The unattainable is attained through its unattainability"). The second, prefacing the first part of the book, is from al-Ḥallādj (whom he called "one of the greatest mystics of mankind"): "To cognise means to see things, but also to see how they are submerged in the Absolute."

From 1917 until seven decades later, Sufism was practically a taboo subject for research. The books and articles written in those years can hardly be regarded as academic. They met, either willingly or unwillingly, the ideological aims of Soviet antireligious state policy.

The theoretical foundation of that policy was Marxist postulates. Accordingly, religion was considered nothing more than "the opium of the people." It is worth noting that, lacking the erudition and intellectual abilities of Marx and Engels, Russian Marxists often appeared fully incapable of understanding or mastering the ideas of their ideological idols. Soviet atheism, in spite of its claim to be scientific, was in fact primitive. Rarely did it reflect individual thinking, doubting, or skepticism;[3] as a rule it demonstrated a servile adherence to imposed dogma. In most cases atheists did not even bother to find out the context of that famous phrase about opium. Many of them would have been surprised to learn that Marx was wise enough to acknowledge:

> Religion is the self-consciousness and a self-esteem of man who has either not yet found himself or has already lost himself again. . . . Religion is the general theory of that world, its encyclopaedic compendium, its logic in a popular form, its spiritualistic *point d'honneur*, its enthusiasm, its moral sanction, its solemn complement, its universal source of consolation and justification. . . . Religion is the sign of the oppressed creature, the heart of a heartless world, just as it is the spirit of spiritless conditions. . . . It is the *opium of* the people. (*Contribution to the Critique to Hegel's Philosophy of Law, Introduction*, p. 145).

The preposition "of" is italicized here to emphasize the fact that Soviet atheists deliberately replaced it with the preposition "for" to underscore the imposed character of religion. It is true that both Marx and Engels overemphasized the negative aspects of the social role religion played. However, they also stated that religions should not be treated as something especially fabricated by "deceivers"; "Religions are founded by people who feel a need for religion themselves and have a feeling for the religious needs of the masses." (F. Engels, *Bruno Bauer and Early Christianity*, p. 429.)

There is no doubt that V. I. Lenin was largely responsible for the introduction of militant atheism.[4] The 'leader of the proletariat of the whole world' did not take any interest in academic studies or theoretical disputes on religion. He did not consider the possibility that religion could "serve the cause of progress." In his mind religion always promoted the justification of social oppression and exploitation. Hence Lenin strongly criticized Kautsky and the other leaders of the 2nd International for treating religion as a private matter, with no concern for either the state of the party's affairs. The leader of the Russian revolution insisted: "So far as the party of the socialist proletariat is concerned, religion is not a private affair. Our Party is an association of class-conscious, advanced fighters for the emancipation of the working class. Such an association cannot and must not be indifferent to lack of class-consciousness, ignorance or obscurantism in the shape of religious beliefs." (V. I. Lenin, *Socialism and Religion*, p. 85.)

The militant atheism of the official ideology that existed in Russia after 1917 restricted religious studies in general and academic studies of mysticism in particular. Adhering to a primitive sociological approach to mysticism, Soviet publications dealt solely with the so-called economic-political roots of the phenomenon, following the marxist distinction between 'progressive' and 'conservative' brands of mysticism. They correlated the former with the antifeudal movements of peasants, and the latter with the mysticism of 'exploiters.'

Two examples demonstrate the typical attitude to mysticism in Russian academic publications of that time. Both are taken from the book that was supposed to be normative—*A Short Dictionary of Scientific Atheism*, prepared at the Institute of Philosophy, USSR Academy of Sciences, and printed by Nauka publishing house in Moscow in 1969. (The second edition of the dictionary had a circulation of 45,000 copies.)

The article on Mysticism asserts:

> mysticism was widespread in the Middle Ages when in accordance with the conditions of the times the revolutionary opposition towards feudalism took the form of mysticism. . . . In modern times it has entirely become the banner of the bourgeois reaction. . . . Mysticism is widely propagated. . . as an imperialist bourgeois ideology aimed against the revolutionary movement. . . . By demonstrating the marasmus of the modern bourgeois ideology and the rejection of scientific cognition of the world by those who serve monopolies, mysticism appears to be one of the striking features of the general crisis of the world capitalist system. (p. 438)

The article on sufism proves to be no less revealing. After announcing that Sufism started in the eighth to ninth centuries among the low stratum of the Muslim clergy as "a movement oriented against social inequality as well as opposed to the cupidity, gluttony and debauchery that reigned among feudals, rich citizens and clerical hierarchs," the article goes on to state that "Sufism demoralized the masses, since by calling upon asceticism, hermitage and self-perfection, the sufis only set up obstacles to the class struggle." The article concludes with the following sentence: "Sufi ideas significantly influenced medieval Persian literature promoting its estrangement from the needs of real life" (p. 667).

It would be unfair to assert that there has been no attempt to present Sufism fairly by crossing these ideological barriers. There were always a few courageous people who dared to be honest. However, their efforts to throw light on the subject were destined to fail due to the overwhelming strength of censorship. Still the blockade was occasionally run by philologists and specialists in the study of literature. The works by Ye. E. Bertels are the most brilliant example of the case in point.

Bertels continued the work started by Zhukovsky. In fact, he studied the writings by the same Persian authors though he was inclined to more generalizations than his predecessor. Bertels was basically the only Russian orientalist who seriously studied Persian Sufism. The collection of his articles on the subject, *Sufism and Sufi Literature*, was highly appreciated by both scholars and common readers.

However, the case of Bertels was not a typical one. The majority of the few writings dedicated to Sufism bore the stamp of Marxist-Leninist hostility to religion and mysticism.

The changes that occurred in the 1980s offered opportunities to study, deliberate about, and express ideas on mysticism as a whole, and on Islamic mysticism in particular, without concern for censorship and hireling critics. The decades-long restrictions on oriental studies in Russia have affected the level of research in this country.[5] There is hope, however, that the day is not far off when Russian works on this intellectually and spiritually inspiring subject will become part of world literature.

This book was conceived at the beginning of the 1970s, when the radical changes in Soviet society were still in the future. I had the opportunity to spend four yeas in Montreal and to work at the library of the Institute of Islamic Studies at McGill University. I used this propitious time for self-education and research on this hitherto practically forbidden subject.

How did Sufism attract my attention? In my more than twenty years of studying nineteenth- and twentieth-century Muslim philosophy and sociopolitical thought, I often wondered how to explain the fact that outstanding Muslim reformers such as Afghānī, Muḥammad ʿAbduh, and Muhammad Iqbal were, at the early stages of their careers, attracted by *taṣawwuf*. These proponents of rational and scientific knowledge in Islamic society turned to irrational teaching. This paradox needed to be explained.

An even more profound motivation to study Sufism was my desire to deviate from ideologically imposed subjects to one that could provide insight into the inner meanings of the Muslim culture hidden behind the coded symbols, metaphors, and allegories.

The Philosophical Aspects of Sufism, published in Moscow in 1987, was, in fact, the signal for running the blockade around the Sufi theme, although the work—especially its introductory and final chapters—was not free from some ideological clichés of bygone times, retained partly for censorship considerations. (The reader must also note that Russian scholars face difficulties in their access to contemporary publications on Sufism.)

Sufism is a most complicated object of study. The combined efforts of researchers in religion and historians, of experts in philology and literature, of psychologists and philosophers are needed to investigate the subject thoroughly. Speaking of his voluminous, 565-chapter work, *Kitāb al-Futūḥāt al-Makkīyya fi maʿrifat al-asrār al-malikīy waʿl-mulkīya* (*The Book of the Revelations Received in Mecca Concerning the Knowledge of the King and Kingdom*) Ibn ʿArabī confessed: "Despite the length and scope of this book, despite the large number of sections and chapters, I have not *exhausted* a single one of the ideas or doctrines put forward concerning the Sufi method" (quoted in H. Corbin, *Creative Imagination*, p. 75; my emphasis). Since a presentation of the theoretical basis of Muslim mysticism proved so formidable a task that even the Great Sheikh found himself unable to cope with it, how much more difficult an undertaking it is to provide an analysis of Sufi ideas. To comprehend them it is necessary to determine their place in the system of Islam, to define the interconnection of Sufism and the main principles of Muslim doctrine, and to compare Sufism with mystical trends in other world religions to find their common and unique traits.

Historical research identifies the social sources of mystical tendencies in Islam, reveals the role of Sufism in the political development of Muslim society, exposes contradictions within its social functions, and recreates the design of its evolution through almost thirteen centuries.

Studies of philologists and specialists in literature contribute to understanding Sufi symbology widely used in Muslim poetry and the ideas underlying the works of Sufi poets and, at the same time, reveal the secrets of mystical apprehension so alluring to the creative nature and to poets in particular.

Psychological investigations of Sufi theory and practices provide an explication of the psychophysiological peculiarities of mystical character and a definition of the autotraining mechanism applied both as a sort of therapeutic device and as a means of delivering the individual from the real troubles of life.

A philosophical study of Islamic mysticism reveals the process of spiritual evolution undergone by Islamic society. Though in the Muslim world the term "philosophy" was associated mainly with Peripateticism, and to a lesser degree with Platonism and Neo-Platonism, the development of philosophy was significantly promoted by religiophilosophic trends, including Sufism, along with Muʿtazila and Ismāʿīlīyya.

The skeptical Sufi attitude to the 'Truth' implanted by theology was not a methodological, cognitive skepticism; still it was a definite spiritual and cultural power of the time that pushed forward philosophic thinking. Sufi irrationality was not always equal to antirationality. "Mystic works of theosophic Sufis are full of criticism of 'rationalists' and of disparagement of reason over against intuition, and *give the impression* that the Sufis are the arch-enemies of philosophy" (F. Rahman, *Islam*. p. 145; my emphasis). However, Sufism was not so much opposed to the rationality of philosophers as to that of theologians, that is, to the legalistic, dogmatic interpretation of the Koran. To be sure, contemplation, direct experience of communion with God, and mystical insight were of primary importance in Sufism, and so chances of rational perception shrank though they never quite disappeared. On the contrary, after al-Ghazālī, a theosophic strain started gaining strength within Sufism that was a synthesis of mystical gnosis and philosophy.

Thus, a study of Sufism as a prominent and influential religiophilosophic trend enables us to reproduce with greater exactitude the process of development and shaping of Muslim philosophy. This places the topic of interest in a much wider historical and philosophical context. Ascertaining Islam's theoretical sources may be helpful in finding out the degree of Islamic mysticism's dependence upon Vedantism, Gnosticism, Neo-Platonism, Zoroastrianism, and Christian mysticism, thus expanding our understanding of the way spiritual influences interact and stimulate each other. Of help also would be the investigation of the influence Sufi ideas have had on the systems of views outside the Muslim world.

This book concentrates on only a few aspects of Sufi philosophy. I am well aware of the relative meaning of the term, "a philosophic credo," as used here, since Sufism has never been a uniform theoretical system. Mystical consciousness as a result of personal perception presupposes the individual character of a mystic experience. To be sure, from the beginning Sufism acknowledged the authority of spiritual preceptors who guide aspirants along the path of attaining the Truth, the 'Reality.' Accordingly, it permitted the existence of different 'schools,' several of which became organized and institutionalized and developed into Sufi orders. Still, for the founders of those orders, as well as for their followers and affiliates, the important thing was practice; emphasis was placed on the ways and methods of achieving mystical experience and not on theorizing about it. Probably the most philosophic trend in Sufism is theosophic mysticism, and "the greatest mystical genius of the Arabs, Ibn ʿArabī" is considered its apostle (A. J. Arberry, *Sufism*, p. 97). Ibn ʿArabī may be called an apostle for he was the first of the Islamic mystics who left a definitive statement (fixed in writing) of Sufi teaching (R. W. J. Austin, *Sufis of Andalusia*, p. 46).[6]

The Great Sheikh, or "the Seal of Muhammadan Sainthood" (the last and the most perfect of Muslim saints) as he called himself, was "the most important link between the Sufis who went before him and those who came after him," for in his writings he expressed and recorded the wisdom of Sufis who preceded him so that "all who came after him received it through the filter of his synthetic expression" (ibid., p. 49). His 'message' found the most splendid representation in the works of Djalāl al-Dīn Rūmī, the great Persian Sufi poet.

Ontological, Gnostic, and ethical views of Ibn ʿArabī and Rūmī have been adduced here in discussing general principles of Sufism[7]—the problems of existence, Man's position in the universe, the ways and chances of attaining comprehension of the Truth, and the criteria of ideal morality and the means of achieving it. The final chapter underscores the role of Sufism in the contemporary world.

As the present study was the first inquiry into the philosophy of Sufism made in the Soviet Union, many of the problems posed necessarily remain unanswered.

The Russian edition had a supplement containing three chapters (chaps. 1, 12, 27) of Ibn ʿArabī's treatise *Fuṣūṣ al-ḥikam* (*The Wisdom of the Prophets*) translated from the Arabic (Beirut ed., 1980), Ḥamza Fansuri's treatise *Asrar al-ʿārifīn* (*The Mysteries of the Gnostics*) written in Sumatra in the early seventeenth century (translated form the Malayan, as published in S. M. N. al-Attas, *the Mysticism of Hamzah Fansuri*, Kuala Lumpur, 1970), Mirza Ghalib's *mathnawī Antimony for the Eyes* (translated from the Farsi *Kulliyyat-e farsi-e Ghalib*, Lahore, 1968), a fragment from Khalil Gibran's *The Garden of the Prophet* (from the London ed., 1974), and three articles by Muhammad Iqbal, published in Urdu in 1916; they appeared in *Waqil*, an Amritsar newspaper, as rebuttals to the critiques of Iqbal's *mathnawī Asrar-i khudī* (*The Mysteries of Personality*) and his preface to it (written in Urdu). The articles are translated from Urdu from a collection of Iqbal's prose works, *Iqbal ke nasri afkar* (Delhi, 1977).

The Supplement was meant to give Russian readers an idea of the Sufi way of thinking and style of expression and also of the adaptation and variation of Sufi notions in the minds and views of twentieth-century essayists and poets. English readers naturally do not need a supplement of this kind as they can read the works mentioned above either in the original or in English translation. *Sufi Wisdom* is a critically revised and enlarged English version published by Ajanta Publications in India in 1989. For those who have access to the vast literature on Sufism in European languages other than Russian, this modest work may be of interest as a "glance from Russia" and as one more point of view on the complex phenomenon of Islamic mysticism.

In the Russian text of this book I translated most quotations from Ibn ʿArabī, Rūmī, and Iqbal from the original Arabic, Farsi, and Urdu. Whenever possible I included the Russian version of the Sufi poets' (Ibn al-Fāriḍ, Ḥāfiẓ, Djāmī, etc.) lines translated in verse by Russian poets. In preparing the present edition for press, available English translations of these Sufi authors were used. The translator considered it best to provide excerpts from European authors in the original accompanied with English translations.

As evidence that the process of in-depth comprehension of the Sufi legacy in the Russian milieu is gaining momentum, and as one more proof that good students standing on their teachers' shouldes can perceive many far-off horizons, synopses of two of my former postgraduate students' theses appear in the appendix: one by A. V. Smirnov on Ibn ʿArabī and the other by K. A. Hromova on S. H. Nasr.

1
Unity of Being

All thou beholdest is the act of one
In solitude, but closly veiled is He.
Let Him but lift the screen, no doubt remains:
The forms are vanished, He alone is all.
Ibn al-Fāriḍ

Ibn ʻArabī, the greatest Master (al-Sheikh al-Akbar), was denominated *Muhyī-d-dīn*, the animator of religion, by some of his contemporaries; others labeled him *Maḥīd-dīn,* he who abolished religion, or even *Mumīt-ud-dīn,* he who kills religion. These contradictory qualifications of one of the most remarkable representatives of Sufism have survived for more than seven centuries, implying and attesting to the complicated nature of this phenomenon and its multifarious roles.

Islamic mysticism has exercised considerable influence on the cultural and sociopolitical life of Muslims. Sufism has been both a product of elite consciousness and a popular religion. It has been a form of social protest against the dominant political system as well as the legalized religious doctrine that warranted and sanctioned the system. Yet Sufism has also been used to quell, to pacify, and to repress social activity. Sufism counterpoised irrationalism to rational thinking while it also stood forth as a variety of religious free-thought not infrequently contiguous with philosophic theorizing. It persuaded seekers of the Path to renounce mundane cares and bodily appetites, to practice ascetic self-discipline, and at the same time it gave inspiration to Niẓāmī, Ḥāfiẓ, Djāmī, Omar Khayam, Rūmī, and many other poets who rapturously extolled love and life.

To determine the sources of the ideas of Islamic mysticism is difficult. Its ideas and images resemble those of other mystical doctrines. For that reason certain researchers in the past (and a few recently) declared Sufism to be a derived, dependent system of ideals and looked for its roots in Neo-Platonism, Zoroastrianism, Buddhism, and the like.

The role of external factors in the rise and development of Islamic mysticism was unduly magnified, partly due to the character of Sufi sources (many of them are in Persian or in languages other than Arabic). Also, the interaction of religious and philosophical theories and doctrines in the Near and Middle East, where the ideas of Christianity, Judaism, and Neo-Platonism had been known long before the Prophet Muḥammad appeared, was underscored.

Yet the mystical world outlook is actually uncircumscribed by any geographical, national, or chronological boundaries. Every religion has its own mystical tradition, and the religious dogmas and tenets determine its peculiar features. While Sufism was subject to external influences as much as the whole of Islam, and was doubtless influenced by various non-Islamic schools, it would be more reasonable to consider Sufism as a product of Muslims' spiritual evolution.

Islamic mysticism is a complicated phenomenon lacking a generally accepted ontological conception. Still, the most prominent idea is the Unity of Being (*waḥdat al-wudjūd*), which presents the culmination of the development of Sufi philosophy[1] (L. Massignon, *Encyclopaedia of Islam*, 4:581)

The idea as such is evident in the earliest philosophic doctrines. Xenophanes of Colophon, Parmenides, Heracleitus, and Anaxagoras (4th–5th cents. B.C.) pondered it; it was further developed by Plato and the Neo-Platonics.

The idea of Unity of Being is the backbone of the famous "Bhagavadgītā":

> There is nothing else besides Me, Arjuna. Like clusters of yarn-beads formed by knots on a thread, all this is threaded on Me.
>
> Arjuna, I am the sapidity in water and the light of the moon and sun; I am the sacred syllable OM in all the Vedas, sound in ether, and manliness in men.
>
> I am pure odour in the earth and pure brilliance in fire; nay, I am life in all beings and austerity in ascetics.
>
> Arjuna, know Me as the eternal seed of all beings. I am the intelligence of the intelligent; the glory of the glorious am I.

In Sufism the concept of the Unity of Being was first formulated by Ibn ʿArabī;[2] consequently its main tenets are articulated by this mystic philosopher of Andalusia and by his followers and commentators.

Ibn ʿArabī's treatises *Fuṣūṣ al-ḥikam* (1230) and *Futūḥāt* (1230–37) are the most representative and popular of his works. The complete title of *All-Futūḥāt* is rendered in English as *The Book of Revelations Received in Mecca Concerning the Knowledge of the King and the Kingdom*. This huge, encyclopeic work evaluated as "a veritable compendium of the esoteric sciences in Islam" (S. H. Nasr, *Three Muslim Sages*, p. 98) contains the life-stories, teachings, and insights of the generations of Sufis who preceded him, and the principles of Sufi doctrines and esoteric sciences.

The compact *Fuṣūṣ al-ḥikam* is, as Ibn ʿArabī himself stated, his most important work as it presents "the kernel" of his philosophy. The title is translated literally as "Bezels of Divine Wisdom," but it is generally paraphrased as "Wisdom of the Prophets." The Arabic noun *fuṣūṣ* (plural of *al-faṣṣ*) denotes the setting that holds the precious stone or the seal of a ring. The "precious stones" of the eternal wisdom mean prophets personifiying different aspects of the Divine knowledge.

Each of the twenty-seven chapters of the treatise is dedicated to one of the prophets mentioned in the Koran, from Adam to

Muḥammad. A few of the names (e.g., Ṣāliḥ, Hūd) are unknown in Judeo-Christian tradition.

The monistic principle of the Unity of Being was considered by Ibn ʿArabī in two planes, which might be called "the cosmic" and "the phenomenal."[3] The Unity of Being is manifested in three levels: the Absolute, the Divine Names (archetypes), and the phenomenal world. To be sure, certain researchers[4] think it proper to distinguish five levels of planes in the system of *waḥdat al-wudjūd* but they find it difficult to describe each plane accurately. Besides, the admission of five planes results from vouchsafing the disparity between Ibn ʿArabī's metaphysical-ontological system and his theological system. The thinker himself spoke repeatedly and clearly enough of the triple division. Thus, in his short treatise *Kitāb Inshā 'al-Dawāʾir* he wrote:

> Know that the things that exist constitute three degrees, there being no other degree of Being. . . . I would assert that of these three (categories) of things the first is that which possesses existence by itself, i.e., that which is existent per se in its very essence. The existence of this thing cannot come from non-Being; on the contrary, it is the absolute Being having no other source than itself. . . . It is, in brief, the absolute Being with no limitations and conditions. Praise be to Him! He is Allah, the Living, the Everlasting, the Omniscient, the One, who wills whatever He likes, the Omnipotent. (Quoted in T. Izutsu, *Sufism and Taoism*, p. 27)

Ibn ʿArabī gives to the Being of the first plane the names of the Absolute, the God, and Reality. "In truth, there is but one single essential Reality (*ḥaqīqa*)" (*Wisdom of the Prophets*, p. 28), "the perfection or the infinity: *al-Kamāl*, in which are 'drowned' all the existential realities as well as the non-existent relations" (ibid., p. 38).

If God is all, what is the world in which we live? "The world is then the shadow of God" (ibid., p. 62). This shadow appeared because God wanted to manifest Himself and thus "to see His own Essence (*al-ʿayn*)" (ibid., p. 8). It is "the sadness of the primordial solitude that makes Him yearn to be revealed. . . suffering anguish in non-knowledge because no one names" His Divine Names. The world, the creation, is the effect of God's yearning to be known (H. Corbin, *Creative Imagination*, p. 184).

Like many other mystics Ibn ʿArabī founds this explication on the *ḥadīth qudsī* (a 'sacred' *ḥadīth*, the authority of which is asserted by Sufis only), stating that when the Prophet David asked God why He had created the world God answered, "I was a hidden treasure, and I wanted to be known, so I created the world." Sufis start with this *ḥadīth* and treat the origin of the world as God's wish to manifest Himself, His hidden Essence. Yet God never manifests Himself completely; He always 'hides' something. "He hides behind the veils of darkness—which are natural bodies—and the veils of light—which are subtle spirits; for the world is made of crude (*ḳathīf*) and other subtle matter (*laṭīf*) (*Wisdom of the Prophets* p. 17). Hindu Vedantism describes very aptly this 'behavior' of God as *lila*, "the sacred pastime," in which the Absolute invests Himself with the cloak (*Maya*).

From the *wudjūdiyya* point of view the Divine act of creation is God's revelation through the created world. Mirza Ghalib, the great poet of Muslim India, expressed this idea in one of his ghazals:

> The world is no more than a manifestation
> of the uniqueness of the Beloved;
> But for the Beauty[5] that seems its own awareness,
> we ourselves would not exist.
> Each place and instant sings, in varying measure,
> a song of being and nonbeing; it is fruitless.
> Wherever his footprint reveals itself, that handful of
> dust is the treaty for the integrity of the two worlds.
> (Mirza Ghalib, *Dīwān*, p. 1)

Creation is a passing from the state of potentiality into the state of revelation, that is, the process of realization of the unconditioned Absolute Divine Being in the world of infinite conditioned potencies.

After division has occurred, so that, while the whole is one; our spirits are a wine and our bodies a vine.
Before it is no 'before', and after it is no 'after'; it is the 'before' of every 'after' by the necessity of its nature.
Its grapes were pressed in the winepress ere Time began and it was an orphan although the epoch of our father (Adam) came after it.

(Ibn al-Farīḍ, quoted in R. A. Nicholson, *Islamic Mysticism*, p. 185).

Two planes of God's revelation are distinguished. The first of these (*at-tadjallī*) is revealed in the Divine Names (*'ilm*), and the other in concrete forms of being of the sensible world. The Divine Names are, "on one hand essentially identical with the Named, and on the other hand, distinct from Him by its particular significance" (*Wisdom of the Prophets*, p. 39). Each Name reveals one of the Divine qualities and differs from all others in its essential determination. It is in the determination that the particular nature, the limitation of each Divine Name belonging to the range of multiplicity are expressed.[6]

The Divine Names form a sphere that is intermediate between the Absolute Being (*wudjūd muṭlaq*) and the limited particular (*wujūd muqayyad*) or phenomenal world. The Names are a sort of link between the Absolute Being and the world, being subject to and dependent on the former and rulers as regards the latter, for the created world is derived from them, is their immediate emanation. Ibn 'Arabī wrote: "We are the fruit of Divine unconditioned generosity towards the Divine Names" (ibid., p. 86). The Divine Names are like light impregnated with the shadow, the Divine shadow projected on the created world. It is by the light that the perception of the shadow takes place. Shadows do not exist in the absence of light; neither is the light possible without the source that produces it.

Ibn 'Arabī made use of complicated Sufi terminology to express his assessment of the universal and the individual. His Divine Names are not only theological categories delineating the Divine attributes but philosophical universals as well. Explicating the interconnection of the universal idea and individual existence and their relation to the Absolute Divine Being, the great Sufi master wrote: "Universal Ideas (*al umūr al-kulliyyah*), which evidently have no individual existence as such, are nonetheless present, intelligibly and distinctly, in the mental state" (ibid., pp. 13–14). And further, "Everything which exists individually emanates from these Ideas, which remain, however, inseparably united to the intellect and could not individually be manifested in such a way as to be removed from the purely intelligible existence" (ibid., p. 14).

The resemblance to Neo-Platonism can be easily traced in Ibn ʿArabī's disquisitions.[7] The Great Sheikh repeatedly underlined that "Universal Ideas, in spite of their intelligibility, have not, as such, their own existence" (ibid., p. 15). Expounding his position he referred to the *universalia humanitatis* and asserted that the universal ideas "are integrally present in everything qualified by them, like humanity (the quality of man), for example, is present integrally in each particular being of this species without undergoing the distinction nor the number which affects individuals, and without ceasing to be in itself a purely intellectual reality" (ibid.).

The Divine Names are the revelation of God in the nonmanifest world of mystery (*ʿālam al-ghayb*) while the phenomenal world is a manifestation of the Divine Being in the world of testimony (*ʿālam al-shahāda*), of objective perception. The Real Absolute Being is God; the world is the manifestation of His Essence. The term *waḥdat al-wudjūd* indicates both the transcendence and immanence of the Absolute Being as regards the phenomenal world.

Affirmation that God is incomparable to things, denial of world's resemblance to God, are decried by Ibn ʿArabī as "ignorance" or lack of tact (*adab*) (ibid., p. 32). He wrote, "The exoterist who insists uniquely on the Divine transcendence (*at-tanzīh*) slanders God and His messengers. . . for he is of those who accept only one part of the Divine revelation and reject the other" (ibid.).

Acceptance of the principle of transcendence leads to dualism, discarding the inherent connection of the general and the particular, of the individual and the many. Contrary to this, the monist adepts of the conception of *waḥdat al-wudjūd* insisted, "Thou art not Him; and yet thou art Him; thou wilt see Him in the essence of things" (ibid., p. 34).

Ḥaydar ʿAlī expressed the relation between God and the world by metaphorically comparing God, or the Absolute Being, to a boundless ocean and concrete things and individual beings to numberless waves or streams differing from the ocean in their definiteness and particularity, yet not diverging from it in their substance and reality. Considered in this sense, the world for Ibn ʿArabī "has not a veritable existence...it is in itself nothing" (ibid., p. 64).

Such statements made certain of the Great Sheikh's opponents and interpreters assume that he considered the world to be a mere illusion existing in the imagination of men. One of the most prominent Sufi opponents of the conception of *waḥdat al-wudjūd*, Sheikh Aḥmad Sirhindī (1564–1624), who set against it the ideas of *waḥat al-shuhūd*, "unity of vision" or "testimonial monism," started with interpreting Ibn ʿArabī's theories in that way. Yet it is memorable that in his later years Sirhindī practically accepted the position of *wudj*ūdiyya and conceded that " in most assertions about reality (*tahqīqāt*) the Sheykẖ is in the right and his detractors far from the truth" (quoted in Y. Friedmann, *Sheikh Aḥmad Sirhindī*, p. 65).

In fact, Ibn ʿArabī continually emphasized the world as created and dependent on the Divine Being. Nonetheless, the world is a manifestation of the Divine Absolute, the realization of the necessary in the casual. "God first created the entire world as something amorphous and without grace (*rūḥ*), comparable to a mirror not yet polished" (*Wisdom of the Prophets*, p. 9). The 'receptacle' produced by God received the inexhaustible effusion of the Divine revelation.

God's manifestations are infinite; hence the boundless variety of the phenomenal world.

Know the world from end to end is a mirror;
In each atom a hundred stars are concealed.
If you pierce the heart of a single drop of water,
From it will flow a hundred dear oceans;
If you look intently at each speck of dust,
In it you will see a thousand beings;
A gnat in its lines is like an elephant;
In name a drop of water rersembles the Nile,
In the heart of a barley-corn is stored an hundred harvests,
Within a millet-seed a world exists.
In an insect's wing is an ocean of life,
A heaven is concealed in the pupil of an eye,
The core in the centre of the heart is small,
Yet the Lord of both worlds will enter there.[8]
(Maḥmūd ash-Shabistarī, *Rose-Garden*, p. 52)

The inexhaustible infinity of indefinitely various forms in which the Divine Being goes on manifesting itself is conditioned by the continuous, uninterrupted process of the Absolute's self-manifestation. "The Divine Order (*al-'amr*) is movement disengaging itself from repose. . . ,the movement of the world from non-existence to existence" (*Wisdom of the Prophets*, pp. 104–5).

The multiplicity of infinitely variegated things in the world is created and derived in contrast with the Absolute Unity of Existence, the Divine Being. This idea was interpreted by Ibn 'Arabī in a way very similar to that of Proclus (410–485), the last of prominent representatives of Greek philosophy—as a dialectic interconnection of the One and the many. In the triad of Proclus it resides in itself, then it goes out of itself, and at last it returns to itself. In the system of *waḥdat al-wudjūd* the Divine Being has neither name or attributes, manifests itself in the phenomenal world, and perpetually strives 'to return' to its primordial state. "The entire reality (*al-'amr*) from its beginning to its end comes from God alone, and it is to Him that it returns" (ibid., p. 10). In terms of Djīlī's metaphor the process is similar to water becoming ice and then water once more (R. A. Nicholson, *Islamic Mysticism*, p. 84).

It is the Perfect Man (*al-insān al-kāmil*) that effects the return to the One and single Essence, and the Perfect Man is considered the most perfect of all beings, the crown and completion of creation. The Perfect Man is to the universe what the bezel is to the seal; he is a sign, a mark engraved on the seal with which God's treasury is guarded. "Man is called the Representative of God, Whose creation he safeguards, as one safeguards the treasury by a seal" (*Wisdom of the Prophets*, p. 12). The world had remained an "unpolished mirror" until God breathed His spirit into Adam, the forefather of Mankind and the Perfect Man as well. In the Koran God says to the angels about Adam, "When I have fashioned him (in due proportion) and breathed into him of My spirit, fall ye down in obeisance unto him" (Sura 15, ayat 29). Ibn ʿArabī took up for comment God's words from another ayat (Sura 38, 75): "O Iblis! What prevents thee from prostrating thyself to one whom I have created with My hands?" (The Arabic noun *biyadayya*, "hands," is used in the form of the dual number.) The thinker interpreted the ayat as evidencing the union in Adam (created with two hands) of the two forms: "the exterior form is created of realities (*ḥaqā'iq*) and of the forms of the world, and the interior form corresponds to the 'Form' of God (that is to say to the 'total' of the Divine Names and Qualities)" (ibid., pp. 17–18).

Man (the genus *Homo*) is the most perfect being in the universe. All other beings are mere reflections of numberless aspects, attributes of the Absolute, while Man's nature synthesizes all the forms of Divine revelation, contains virtually all other natures created (ibid., p. 12) and "receives in himself all the different Essential realities (*ḥaqā'iq*) which constitute the world" (ibid., p. 86). Still, since the world in its entirety is the macrocosm (*ʿālam-i-akbar*), Man is the microcosm (*ʿālam-i-asgar*). In other words, the principle of the Unity of Being obtains in the phenomenal world just as consistently. If on the cosmic level the Unity of Being means in fact that "All is God," on the phenomenal level the Unity of the Absolute means "All is Man."

> Therefore in form thou art the microcosm,
> Therefore in reality thou art the macrocosm.
> (Rūmī, *Mathnawī*, Book 4, 521)

The idea of macrocosm and microcosm is not to be found in Sufism only. Anaximenes, Pythagoras, Heracleitus, Empedocles, and other Greek philosophers up to the Stoics and Neo-Platonists held the concept. It is also found in the theories of the Orphics and Gnostics. A similar concept of the Universum is typical of taoism in which Man is contemplated as system not just analoguous or similar to that of cosmos but identical with it both structurlly and essentially. The idea was expressed by Muslim thinkers before Ibn ʿArabī. Thus al-Ghazālī, interpreting the *ḥadīth* "God created Adam in His form," maintained that Man was created in the semblance of the macrocosm but as its diminished variety and that Adam's component parts were similar to the component parts of the macrocosm.

Primitive Man did not distinguish himself from his natural environment. This was largely due to a "natural economy" way of life. Man found in nature a continuance of his ego and the clan and tribe social relations. In the Middle Ages Man no longer blended with nature. In that period, as prominent Russian scholar A. Ya. Gurevich writes, Man no longer assumed an attitude toward the world as object but rather comprehended himself in the exterior world and apprehended the cosmos as the subject. Discovering a sequence of himself in the world he elicited the universe in himself. Man and universe discerned each other (*Categorii*, p. 69).

The concepts of macrocosm and microcosm were widespread in medieval times, yet they frequently had different connotations with unique accents. It is easy to trace in the opinions of Ibn ʿArabī and his adherents an endeavor to override the dualistic worldview (typical of the Middle Ages in general and of Muslim mentality in particular) that accepted the existence of both the Divine world and the sensible world associated (especially by Christians) with the world of evil, of the devil's malevolence.

In the *waḥdat al-wudjūd* system Man is not only a microcosm viewed as an epitome, a measure of the universe, of the whole world of being, of the macrocosm, but as something incomparably more significant, as an intermediate link between God and the phenomenal world, thus ensuring the unity of cosmic and phenomenal being.

The monism of this system is summarized most plainly by Ibn ʿArabī: "From its existential unity, the shadow is God himself, for God is the Unique (*al-wāḥid*), the One (*al-aḥad*); and in respect of the multiplicity of sensible forms, it is the world" (*Wisdom of the Prophets*, p. 64). The Divine Essence is the immanent cause of all being; it is eternal and at the same time perpetually manifesting itself in an unfathomable number of creatures.

Waḥdat al-wudjūd belongs to the variety of religio-philosophical doctrines that may be defined a mystical pantheism.[9] Contrary to the naturalistic pantheism that dissolves God in nature, its maxim being "God is all,"[10] mystical pantheism dissolves nature in God, insisting on the principle "All is God." Still, the qualifications of Ibn ʿArabī's and his adherents' Sufi views as a pantheistic doctrine has been confuted. Most ostentatious is the position of S. H. Nasr, F. Schuon, and other modern promulgators of Sufism. Nasr, for example, disclaims such classification as depreciative and declaims 'accusations' of pantheism as false (*Three Muslim Sages*, pp. 104–5).

Nasr argues that "pantheism is a philosophical system" while Sufi views, and those of Ibn ʿArabī in particular, are not any philosophy at all for they (Sufis) "never claimed to follow or create any 'system' whatsoever," their way of thinking being merely "Islamic esoterism," Gnostic knowledge. Both Nasr and Schuon take it for granted that metaphysics and Gnostic theories are outside the sphere of philosophy since "a metaphysical doctrine is the incarnation in the mind of a universal truth. . . . A philosophical system is a rational attempt to resolve certain questions which are put to ourselves" (*Understanding Islam*, p. 11).

Of more importance is Nasr's insistence that while "pantheism implies a substantional continuity between God and the universe" Ibn ʿArabī claims "God's absolute transcendence over every category, including that of substance" (*Three Muslim Sages*, p. 105); "it is true that God dwells in things but the world does not 'contain' God" (ibid.). Nasr does not accept the possibility that there are different varieties of pantheism.

The vulnerable point of Ibn ʿArabī's pantheistic position is his acceptance of the act of creation; nature and Man are created by God, the Absolute, who is above all qualities. In Ibn ʿArabī's treatise *Fuṣūṣ al-ḥikam* creationist ideas, while subtle, are nonetheless present: "God first created the entire world" (*Wisdom of the Prophets*, p. 9); "Man is. . .a being created perpetual and immortal" (ibid., p. 12).

The pantheism of *waḥdat al-wudjūd* is manifested in religio-mystical ideas. While the thesis "God is all" may logically lead to materialism (as, for example, in Spinoza who started with a pantheistic tradition), the thesis "All is God" limits the chances of such an approach. God is, then, essentially the same as the world but infinitely more 'voluminous': "I am God," but "God is not I." As Ibn al-Fāriḍ says:

> I was ever She, and She was ever I, with no difference;
> nay, my essence loved my essence.
> I was nothing in the world except myself beside me,
> and no thought of beside-ness occurred to my mind.
>
> If I recant my words, 'I am She', or if I say—and
> far be it from one like me to say it!—that She became
> incarnate (*ḥallat*) in me, (then I shall deserve to die
> and death).
> (Quoted in R. A. Nicholson, *Islamic Mysticism*, pp. 224–25)

Man's pretension of being the same as God, expressed in the famous utterance "*anā'l-Ḥaqq*" (I am the Absolute Truth") for which Manṣūr al-Ḥallādj paid with his life since it was a direct challenge to the Islamic religious system, was amended by Ibn ʿArabī. He substituted the formula "I am God's secret" (or, "I am His shadow," a theophany) for that of *anā'l-Ḥaqq* and refuted "their pretension of identification with God" (*Wisdom of the Prophets*, p. 54).

The amendment of Ḥallādj's formula caused certain researhers to disbelieve the monistic nature of *waḥdat al-wudjūd*. The doubts seem unfounded since those who upheld the concept of the Unity of Being, though they specified difference between the Absolute and His phenomenal form, between God and the world, did insist on their substantial unity.

The monism of *waḥdat al-wudjūd* consists in admitting the principle of subject/object identity, according to which the subject is not secondary to the object (substance) but *a mode of its existence*. It is for the self-revelation of the One that the development of an identical principle takes place; God, the self-conscious reason, may be manifested only in Man's perception of nature and of the world: "the ephemeral being manifests the 'form' of the eternal." God, wishing to see Himself, manifests Himself in the ephemeral world. "In contemplating Him we contemplate ourselves, and in contemplating ourselves He contemplates Himself" (ibid., p. 16).

Within the medieval spiritual culture of Islam the religious philosophy of Sufism stood in a certain contraposition to both traditional Islamic doctrine and the worldview of the adherents of *falsafa*—Muslim Peripatetics. In the ontological shpere this contrast was expressed in the opposition of Sufi monistical pantheism to theism, on the one hand, and to the naturalistic pantheism, on the other.

Theism presupposes the transcendence of God, the Creator of the world and its perpetual Ruler. Within Islam theism was realized either in sharp dual division (the substance, God, and the nonsubstantial, the world; or God, the High Substance, and the world, a created, lower substance) or in the plurlism of *kalām* atomistics.

Until recently it was generally accepted in Islamology that it was mutakallimūn's atomistics that formed the ontological basis of Muslim scholastic theology.[11] Lately an attempt to refute that point of view has been undertaken by a number of Arabian scholars, including Kh. Muruiwe, T. Tizini, and T. Kh. Ibrahim. Whatever variations occur in the interpretation of *kalām*, the atomistic principle of its ontological system has not been called into question on the whole. The question remains, however, whether the atomism of *kalām* had a theistic orientation (as historians of philosophy traditionally believe) or a pantheistic tinge (as T. Kh. Ibrahim, for one, has tried to prove).

Mutakallimun's atomistics might be called pantheistic if the thesis of T. Kh. Ibrahim is accepted, namely, that "in philosophical pantheism God is not only immanent to the universe but also necessarily transcendent to it" (*Philosophia Kalama*, p. 19). Yet objections must be raised against this very thesis. First, the generally accepted view is incomparably better grounded: the main distinction of pantheism from theism consists in the latter's acceptance of God's transcendence (S. S. Averintsev, *Filosofskaya entsiklopedia*, 189). This acceptance appearing alongside pantheistic views merely testifies to the perfunctory and confutable nature of such views.[12]

Second, Sufis in fact recognized God's immanence and transcendence at the same time. But adepts of *waḥdat al-wudjūd* confined this view mainly to the sphere of cognition while their position in ontology was consequential and they maintained the pantheistic thesis of God's immanence as regards nature.

In Ash'arīyya's atomistics, the main and dominating feature was the idea of God's transcendence over nature (even though this idea might coexist sometimes with the idea of God's immanence). According to mutakallimūn "The Universe, that is, everything contained in it, is composed of very small parts which are indivisible." Unlike atomists of ancient Greece, Ash'arīyya believed that "these atoms are not . . . numerically constant, but are created anew whenever it pleases the Creator" (Maimonides, *Guide for the Perplexed*, pp. 120–21).

Objects have no inherent attributes; attributes are accidental and created anew by God. "God creates a substance and simultaineously its accidents. . . . He can of His will create in the same subsance an accident of a different kind" (ibid., p. 124). When a man is writing it is not he who really moves a pen; the motion produced in the pen and in the hand is an accident God has created. The conclusion of mutakallimūn is as follows: "There does not exist anything to which an action can be ascribed, the real *agent* is God" (ibid., p. 125). One cannot doubt the theistic nature of the formulas just quoted.[13]

Muslim philosophers were well aware of this and adverted to it. Referring to Abū Nasr al-Fārābī, whose views he shared, Ibn Rushd wrote that mutakallimun asserted the existence of potentiality in the only Maker, in the Absolute Demiurge, whose creative act was in no need of primordial matter; they believed that they had proved the creatio ex nihilo (see *Guide for the Perplexed*, p. 178). Thus it was that Sufism (*waḥdat al-wudjūd*) with its pantheistic monism came into conflict not only with the unreserved theism of Islamic traditionalists (Ḥanbalīs, Ẓāhiriyya, Salafiyya, etc.) but with the theism of *kalām* as well. Of special interest here is the example of al-Ghazālī in whose doctrine the ideas of Ashʿarīyya were joined to those of Sufism and who, nonetheless, refuted mystical pantheism and ranked its adepts (it was Manṣūr al-Ḥallādj he had in mind) among extreme fanatics who spread the bounds of conformity up to unity (*Voskresenie*, p. 250).

Still the ontological views of Sufis (adepts of *waḥdat al-wujūd* in particular), with all their digressions from the orthodox Islamic doctrine, remained within the bounds of a religious worldview. The philosophical potentials of pantheism were not and could not be fully realized since Sufi pantheism was mystical. It did attempt, however, to give a philosophic interpretation of Islamic monotheism. The very fact that Sufis endeavored proves they made a step toward a philosophic worldview and, consequently away from religious dogmatism. It is not by chance that Ibn Sīnā, the prominent representative of *falsafa*, called Sufis "his brothers in search of the Truth."[14]

The relation between Sufism and *falsafa* is very complicated and contradictory. In particular, the role of Sufism in the evolution of philosophic thinking in Islamic countries deserves a more adequate evaluation. It is well known that ancient Greek philosophy, primarily Aristotelian philosophy, had great influence on the development of philosophy in the Near and Middle East. The impact of Aristotelians was so great as to induce the creation of the oriental Peripatetic school represented by such promnent thinkers as al-Kindī (ca. 800–ca. 870), al-Fārābī (870–950), Ibn Sīnā (980–1037), and Ibn Rushd (1126–98). The fact that Peripatetic doctrines carried the name of "*falsafa*" does not mean, to be sure, that other schools (Muʿtazila, Ismāʿīlīyya, Sufism) were exempt from participation in the development of philosophy in the Muslim world throughout the Middle Ages. It shows only that oriental

Peripatetics who continued and extended the traditions of ancient Greek spiritual culture on their soil, naturally, were apprehended by their compatriots as representatives of that kind of thinking for which there was no name in Arabic until it was coined from the Greek word "philosophy" (deformed into *falsafa*). Besides, Aristotelianism was clearly distinguished from the dominate religious worldview due to its elements of materialism and pronounced rationalism.

Researchers have not been able to agree about the problems of the genesis and the peculiar nature of the oriental Peripateticism. For a long time there prevailed in European scholarship the opinion that philosophy in Arabic was completely epigonic, devoid of originality altogether. Hegel asserted that Arab philosophy had not formed a particular stage of its own in the general course of the development of philosophy, nor had it furthered in any way the principle of philosophy ("Ihre Philosophie macht nicht eine eigentumliche Stufe in der Philosophie; sie haben das Prinzip der Philosophie nicht weiter gebraucht" [*History of Philosophy*, Bd. 19, S. 125]). According to Ernest Renan, "Arabs did nothing but adopt the whole of Greek encyclopaedic thought just as all the world had accepted it by the seventh and eighth centuries" ("Les Arabes ne firent qu'adopter l'ensemble de l'encyclopedie grecque, telle que le monde entier l'avait acceptee vers le VIIe et le VIIIe siecle" [*Averroès*, p. ii. Avertissement pour le 4e edition]). A sharper qualification was offered by Ignaz Goldziher, a famous orientalist: "From the outset the Arabic philosophy was marked—due to absolute deficiency of critical ability—with the stamp of eclecticism evident in all the directions of its development" (Der vollige Mangel kritischer Fahigkeit druckte von allem Anfang der Arabischer Philosophie den Stempel des Eklektizismus auf der sich in jede der Richtigungen in denen sied sich entfaltet hat, in unverkennbarer Weise bekundet" [*Die Islamische Philosophie*, S. 52]).

Research in the history of philosophy in recent decades has introduced vital correctives into the understanding of oriental Peripateticism and prompted certain novel conclusions. In fact, the doctrines developed by the Muslim Peripatetics were founded on "Neo-Platonic" Aristotelianism. The formal reason for that is easy to find in the circumstances of Aristotle's ideas penetrating into that region. Arabs first learned of them from two books translated into Arabic on the initiative of al-Kindī 'the philosopher of Arabs.' The first treatise was the so-called Theology of Aristotle, which contained certain fragments from the *Enneads* (the fourth to the sixth) of Plotinus as well as several texts by Aristotle; the second, called "The Book of Causes," contained the *Elements of Theology* by Proclus.

Further development was not an outgrowth of false reasoning, credulity, ignorance, or 'lack of critical ability.' The adoption of Neo-Platonic (not of 'pure') Aristotelianism was conscious and premeditated, dictated by the needs and circumstances of the Muslim world. Still, it would be incorrect to insist that it was the commixture of Aristotelianism and Neo-Platonism that specified the oriental Peripateticism (A. V. Sagadeev, *Ibn-Sina*, pp. 62ff.). It is in Plotinus' writings and in those of Proclus and other Neo-Platonists that one can distinguish integration of Plato's and Aristotle's ideas. The systhesis was adopted by Muslim philosophers, who mastered it and managed to realize its further transformation. The creative elaboration of the material embraced proceeded not (as some investigators prefer to think) by way of expurgating Aristotelianism from Neo-Platonic depostions but in the course of modifying both Plato's and Aristotle's ideas. Medieval Islam thinkers who tended to prove the independence of philosophical and scientific knowledge were especially drawn to Aristotle's logic, his theoretical discrimination of the Essence, the empirical trend of his gnoseology, and his natural philosophy. Their veneration of the "first master's" prominence did not portend, however, any blind imitation. Al-Fārābī, who gained the appellation of "the second master," declared that following the example of Aristotle should be such that love for him would never surpass the adherence to truth (*Filosofskie tractaty*, p. 13).

Arabic-speaking Peripatetics gave preference to the Truth and reconsidered the heritage of Aristotle using Neo-Platonic ideas, primarily the principle of emanation. Adverting to this principle was necessary and expedient in view of the position of its direct ideological adversary, theological creationism. It was by using the principle of emanation that Aristotle's doctrine of the Thinking Mind, the main link in the system of his philosophy, could be transformed and thus the premises formed for treating Being as unified and dynamic, laying the foundation for a truly philosophic worldview that might be opposed to the theological treatment of existence with its separation of the universe into two parts, the "Creator" and the "creation."

In Arabic Peripateticism the Greek *to prōton* kinoyn is supplanted by the Primary Cause. Al-Fārābī wrote that the Being of the Primary Essence is a sort of emanation of Being into being of other things, while the being of everything else emanates from His own Being. The principle of emanation is not a fortuitous Neo-Platonic accretion in Arabic systems but their organic component. To be sure beforehand it had to be reconsidered and modified on the basis of the ample experience of natural philosophers of the East. The development of this principle in the spirit of philosophical or natural pantheism was manifest from al-Fārābī until Ibn Rushd.

Ibn Rushd, like other Peripatetics, called the Supreme permanent Principle "Reason divorced from matter." For Averroes Reason was the harmony and order present in all things, the order and the harmony apprehended by active powers that are in possession of order and harmony since they exist in all beings called 'natures' by philosophers.

The Great Cordovan thinker's consistent monism found expression in naturalistic pantheism, in assertin the Unity of Being and the immanence of the form to matter. Thus the principle of emanation, common with all Easter Peripatetics and Sufis and forming the premises for the foundation of the idea of God's and the universe's unity, further bifurcated in the direction of naturalistic pantheism (in Peripatetics) and of mystical pantheism (in Sufis).

Peripatetics' attitude to Sufis may be characterized by two impressive examples from the life-stories of Ibn Sīnā and Ibn-Rushd. Tradition holds that after conversing with Abū Sa'īd Mayhāna, an eminent Persian Sufi, the philosopher said, "All that I know he sees," while the mystic described their encounter with the words, "All that I see he knows." Tradition seems quite trustworthy, especially when compared with the facts from Ibn Rushd's life told by Ibn ʿArabī in his treatise *Futūḥat*.

The Great Sheikh asserts that Averroes, having heard of his mystical experience, expressed the disire to meet him, then a young man of twenty, personally and Ibn ʿArabī's father arranged the interview. At this meeting the beardless Sufi, the famous philosopher, looked at him with consideration and said, "Yes." The answer was "Yes" and Ibn Rushd was satisfied seeing that the young man had understood what was in his mind. But then the Sufi added, "No." Immediately Averroes winced; the color went out of his cheeks; he seemed to doubt his own thought and asked, "What manner of solution have you found through divine illumination and inspiration? Is it identical with that which we obtain from speculative reflection?" And Ibn ʿArabī replied, "Yes and no" (quoted in H. Corbin, *Creative Imagination*, pp. 41–42).

These encounters deserve mention for they show that both philosophers and Sufis were conscious of similarity and differnce in their views. They maintained, in common, the monistic unity of being, notwithstanding the difference mentioned above, for Peripatetics comprehended the Unity of Beng in the spirit of naturalistic pantheism ("God is the sum of existence") while Sufis were inclined to consider everything as derived from God. The heterogeneity of their ontological views was mainly due to the difference of methods through which they came to comprehend the Unity of Being. The monistic deduction of philosophers resulted from their scientific experience and rationalistic speculation, while the *waḥdat al-wudjūd* was prompted by intuition, by exalted feelings of men perceiving in mystical experience their integral unity with nature and its creator.

2

Anguish after the Hidden

The sages gain their deepest lore by wine's resplendent light
The inward gem of everyone this ruby brings to light.
None but the bird interprets well the volume of the rose,
Not every reader of a leaf its latent import knows.

Ḥāfiẓ

A Sufi takes as axiomatic God's existence as Absolute Being, His pervading the universe, and the Unity of Being. The Sufi mind is mainly busy with the problems of the possibilities and limitations of knowledge and with the ways and methods of achieving the insight of Truth. Hence researchers investigating Sufi ontological views possess scarce 'illustrative' material (it was not by chance that in elucidating Sufi ontology in the preceding chapter, I had to rely mainly on statements of Ibn ʿArabī, the most speculative, probably, of Sufi thinkers[1]), while scholars who undertake an analysis of the cognitive views of Muslim mystics can appeal not only to their treatises but to their immense poetic heritage as well.

Can the Truth, the essence of the Absolute Being, be grasped? That is the cardinal problem for Sufis and the answer is not pure and simple; it is both yes and no.

God, the Absolute Truth, cannot be conceived by the human mind. The incomprehensibility of Being is in agreement with the ontological treatment of the universe as God's revealing of Himself. "The world does not participate in the autonomy of the Essential

Being, so much so that it can never conceive Him. *In this respect* God remains always unknown, to the intuition as well as to the contemplation, for the ephemeral has no hold on the eternal" (*Wisdom of the Prophets*, p. 17; my emphasis).

Sense perception and concepts of reason based on sensory experience are unable to discover the Truth:

> Reason is the shadow of God; God is the sun:
> what power hath the shadow to resist His sun?
> (Rūmī, *Mathnawī*, 4:389.)

Sufis employ similes like Plato's 'cave' (*Republic* 6.514a–517d) when they talk about the dubious and illusory nature of sensory-rationalistic knowledge. Djalāl al-Dīn Rūmī's *Mathnawī* contains a parable about an elephant inside a dark barn. The people there tried to find out what it was by fumbling and groping. One grabbed the trunk and declared it was a waterpipe; another touched an ear and concluded it was a huge fan; the third stumbled at the elephant's legs and supposed them to be columns; the fourth felt its back and declared it was a big throne. The conclusion of the parable is that the information supplied by human sense organs is superficial and false. Human reason relying on the data of sense organs and taking it as trustworthy is sure of falling into error. One of ghazals in Mirza Ghalib's *Dīwān* (p. 88) expresses this:

> Deceptive is devotion to the magic 'shadow-shapes',
> which form the illusive appearance of all we hear and see.
> Their myriad forms of beauty make an infidel of me:
> I seek the outward forms and lose the vision of unity.

Another ghazal deals with the import of utterance:

> The relation of sense and sound, import and speech
> Is the relation of kernel and husk
> Which must peel off to show the shell within. (Ibid., p. 28)

The perceptions of our senses and the conclusions of our reason are fallacious since what appears to them is merely the shadow and not that which casts it, merely the phenomenal and not the essential. Our senses and reason are aware of the multiplicity but unable to secure cognition of the one single Reality.

> I gained by fealty to her neither by hearing nor by sight
> nor by acquisition nor by the attraction of my nature,
> But I was enamoured of her in the world of command, where
> is no manifestation.
>
> (Ibn al-Fāriḍ, *Tā'iyyat*, p. 214)

The deception of the testimony of sensory-rational experience is also due to the accessory impact of the 'subjective factor.' Man can percive with his senses only the image of the Absolute's self-manifestation, 'God's shadow.' But God projects this shadow on its place of manifestation, which Ibn ʿArabī compares to "a filter of coloured glass, which tints the light to its own colour whereas it is itself without colour" (*Wisdom of the Prophets*, p. 64).

Sufi thinkers (thinkers, not mere representatives of Sufi orders, of the institutionalized Sufism) never denied the validity of rational knowledge even though they recognized its limited possibilities. Rūmī said, "Reason is excellent and desirable until it brings you to the door of the King. Once you have reached His door, divorce reason;. . .surrender yourself to Him; you have no use then for how and wherefore" (*Discourses of Rumi*, pp. 122–23).

One should also keep in mind that Sufis attacked reason because they felt aversion for the rationalistic official theology. Muslim reformers of the twentieth century, Muhammad Iqbal in particular, spoke of Sufism as fostering "a kind of revolt against the verbal quibbles of our early doctors" and qualified it as "a form of free thought in a alliance with rationalism" (*Reconstruction*, p. 150).

The object of Sufi cognition was limited by the religious sphere. They were mainly concerned with seeking answers to the questions: What is God? What is Man? Is it possible to attain the knowledge of God? How does one proceed on the Path? What should Man be guided by in his daily behavior? While Muslim theologians discussed the Islamic doctrine in literal accordance with the phrases of the Koran and Sunna, having recourse to logical devices besides, Sufis sought for the sense hidden in the Prophet's revelation, the sense corresponding to their personal views and states of mind. As W. C. Chittick rightly points out, "many Sufis set up their teachings in contradiction to those of the jurists (*fuqahā'*) or the dogmatic theologians (the specialists in *kalām*). Hence they are critical of the juridical and theological perspectives, and it is easy to assume that they themselves wanted to have nothing to do with these 'exoteric' sciences. But the issue was rather one of establishing the right sort of priorities. Sufis did not deny the legitimacy of these sciences, merely the exaggerated claims for authority made by many of their practitioners" (*Faith and Practice*, p. xiii).

The knowledge of Muslim theologians was, according to Rūmī, the science of the King's (God's) edicts while Sufis tried to master the science of the Ruler. "What is knowledge of the science of the edicts, compared with knowing the science of the Ruler?" (*Discourses of Rumi*, p. 113). The poet protested against such imperfect knowledge foisted upon believers and exclaimed wrathfully,

> Blind imitation of them has brought me to ruin:
> two hundred curses be on that imitation!
>
> (*Mathnawī*, 2:251)

And again,

> Know that beside the breath (words) of the Quṭb[2] of
> the time traditional knowledge is like performing the
> ritual ablution with sand when there is water (available).
>
> (Ibid., 4:35.)

Rational knowledge is imperfect when compared with 'direct' attainment of the Truth achieved only in mysterious experience. Such experience is always personal, individual; still it has certain features common to both Sufism and other mystical traditions. The very moment of realizing the Truth, of attaining it, comes suddenly like a 'dazzling light.' Dante thus describes his vision in the final lines of his "Paradiso":

> Tale era io a quella vista nuova:
>   Veder voleva, come si convenne
>   L'imago al cerchio, e come vi s'indova,
> Ma non eran da ciò le proprie penne.
>   Se non che la mia mente fu percossa
>   Da un fulgore, in che sua voglia venne.
>
>   Even such was I at that ne apparition;
> I wished to see how the image to the circle
> Conformed itself, and how it there finds place;
>   But my own wings were not enough for this,
> Had it not been that then my mind there smote
> A flash of lightning, wherein came the wish.
> (*Divine Comedy*, pp. 162–63)

Sufis frequently associate this dazzling light with a fire or a flame as we see, for example, in the following lines of Ḥāfiẓ:

> Show us Thy face, and at the same time say:
> "Moths of my candle, be prepared to die."
> (*Selections* p. 120)

The releasing power of intuition is contrasted with the sluggishness of reason incapable of attaining the Truth.[3]

Science does not deny the cognitive role of intuition although assessing it in an absolutely different way from mysticism. However, great the variety of explanations proffered, it is generally agreed that the main, essential part of intuition is "immediate apprehension," immediate knowledge of the truth in a proportion not preceded by inference, a hunch, a flash of insight (*Encyclopaedia of Phlosophy*, Vol. 4, p. 204}. Yet the immedicacy is relative, conditional. When he criticized Friedrich Heinrich Jacobi, Hegel drew attention to the fact that immediate knowledge was always mediated, determined: "Das unmittelbare Wissen ist so ubarall vermittelt" (*History of Philosophy*, Bd. 19, S. 549. Vorlesungen über die Geschichte der Phislosophie, Bd. 3, Theil 3, Abschnitt 3, A), and that "The sphere of Essence thus turns out to be a still imperfect combination of immediacy and mediation" (*Philosophy of the World History*, p. 211). Hegel did not give a complete explanation of the notion of 'mediation.' It remained for him and it could not be, in fact, anything more than the mediation of an idea by an idea, of a notion by a notion.

Within Sufism, intuition—as pure imagination, devoid of any mediation whatever—ran counter to insistence on following the *Ṭarīqa*, the 'Path,' the 'Way,' which meant spiritual education, supervised by a master (sheikh) who transmitted to adepts a certain sum of knowledge, striving to attain moral perfection by means of ascetic practices and mastery of a special system of psychophysical exercises. Thus it was that while asserting the immediacy of insight mystics never ceased to propound the necessity of preparation for it. Al-Ghazālī explained in the fourth part of his *Iḥyā' 'ulūm ad-din* (*Revival of the Religious Sciences*), in its ninth book on "Meditation" that knowledge comes sometimes from the Divine Light in Man's heart related to the natural disposition (*fitr*), as is the case with prophets, and sometimes (and more frequently) through learning and discipline.

From the viewpoint of science the preparation for intuitive enlightenment is realized by means of practice, experiment and, at last, logical conclusions. Jules Henri Poincaré, a famous French mathematician (1854–1912), telling of his own experience (in his report on creative work in mathematics quoted at length by J. Hadamard) remarked, "Most striking at first is this *appearance* of sudden illumination, a manifest sign of long, unconscious prior work. The role of this unconscious work in mathematical invention appears to me incontestable." He added that "sudden inspirations. . .never happen except after some days of voluntary effort" (*Mathematical Creation*, pp. 14, 45; my emphasis).

The specific character of mystics' preparation for intuitional realization is mainly dependent on their orientation, on the primary aim of Sufi quest for Truth. The term "intuition" comes from the Latin word *intuitio*, which means literally "looking intently." A scientist concentrates on the phenomena and objects of the external world. An artist or philosopher perceives "the inner depth of his spirit" ("die Tiefen des Gemuths und Geistes"), as Hegel used to say, directing his mental eye at the internal and the external world ("durch die Richtung des eigenes Geistes auf die innere und aussere Welt" [*Werke*, Bd. 10, S. 36]). Mystical intuition ('spiritual insight') is oriented at looking into oneself, self-analysis and self-consciousness.

> Into my heart's night along a narrow way
> I groped; and lo! the light, an infinite land of day.
> (Rūmī, *Dīwān*. Quoted in
> A. J. Arberry, *Sufism*, p. 117)

Sufi gnoseology makes a hermeneutical circle, with its logic of moving from subjectivity to substantionality, from Man's perception of himself to his perception of God, and again returning from the general to the particular.

In Rūmī's *Mathnawī* there is a parable about a Sufi who came into a fine orchard and, instead of enjoying the beauty of nature sat on the ground and laid his head upon his knees. His friend was bewildered: "Why, doest thou sleep. Nay, look at the vines, behold these trees and . . . green plants. . . . Turn thy face towards these marks of Divine Mercy!" He replied, "Its marks are within the heart. That which is without is only the mark of the marks" (4:1358–62). Alexander of Macedon in Djāmī's *Book of Iskandar's Wisdom* gives similar edifying advice:

> Beware! . . . Thou are but the glass,
> And He the face confronting it which casts
> Its image in the mirror. . . If steadfastly
> Thou canst regard, thou wilt at length perceive
> He is the mirror also.
> (Quoted in E. G. Brown, *Literary History*, 2:439)

It might seem that the way of attaining the Truth through self-knowledge is in opposition to the bidding of self-renunciation, of annihilation of the personal ego so persistntly enjoined by Muslim mystics. In fact, there is no incongruity at all for it is the phenomenal ego that must be forgotten and annihilated so that the real, the essential self can be revealed.

> Therefore mortify thyself that thou mayst behold in thee and from thee a peace beyond what I have described—a peace born of a feeling of calm.
> After my self-mortification I saw that he who brought me to behold and led me to my (real) self was I; nay, that I was my own example.
> And that my standing (at 'Arafāt) was a standing before myself; nay, that my turning (towards the Ka'ba) was towards myself. Even so my prayer was to myself and my Ka'ba from myself.
>
> (Ibn al-Fāriḍ, *Tā'iyyat*, pp. 221–22).

The medieval poet-Sufi sang the necessity of getting free from the mundane husk concealing the kernel self, the microcosm. He enumerated hindrances—human passions, lay superstitions due to tendencies prevailing in the society, injunctions of official theology—all that kept Man from knowing his own self and hence the Divine Real Self. A prominent ninth-century Sufi, Bāyazīd Bisṭāmī, wrote,

> I shed myself away as a snake sheds its skin.
> I looked into my essence and. . .Oh I became Him.

Sufis used symbols generally employed in the universal mystical literature; thus they compared Man's self to a house that had to be cleansed or even taken down and then rebuilt so that the true self might be manifested:

> I am a house, but a house forsaken since time immemorial.
> To be exonerated from the curse
> It must be cleansed, restored and renovated,
> And plastered over with the clay of God's Grace.

This quatrain from the "Lamentations" of the great Armenian poet Grigor Narekatsi (951–1003), a Christian mystic, harmonizes with the lines from Djalāl al-Dīn Rūmī's *Mathnawī* written two hundred years later:

> . . . Ruined the house for the sake of the golden treasure,
> and with that same treasure builds it better than before;
> Cut off the water and cleansed the river-bed, then caused
> drinking-water to flow in the river-bed. (2:20)

Sufis emphasize the idea's accordance with the spirit of the sacred book of Muslims and quote the Koran (Sura 33, ayat 72)—"We did indeed offer the trust to the Heavens and the Earth and the Mountains, but they refused to undertake it, being afraid thereof: but man undertook it"—taking the ayat as a proof of Man's predestination to be the receptacle of the Divine Essence. Man's ignorance is due to the fact that he has forgotten his high predestination and has looked for the treasure of Truth everywhere except within himself. The path to the knowledge of God should take Man through rejection of his external self to affirmation of his real self:

> O you who possess sincerity, if you want that (Reality)
> unveiled, choose death and tear off the veil—
> Not such a death that you will go into a grave, but a death
> consisting of (spiritual) transformation, so that you
> will go into Light.
>
> (Rūmī, *Mathnawī*, 6:299)

The death of the phenomenal self opens the way to the essential knowledge in which there is no distinction of subject and object and the Truth of the Unity of Being is attained.

> He is thou, but not this (unreal) 'thou': (He is) that
> 'thou' which in the end is conscious of escape (from the
> world of illusion).

Thy last (unreal) 'thou' has come to thy first (real)
'thou' to receive admonition and gifts.
Thy (real) thou is buried in another (unreal 'thou')
(Ibid., 6:466)

The Truth is yourself, but not your mere bodily self,
Your real self is higher than 'you' and 'me'.
This visible 'you' which you fancy to be yourself
Is limited in place, the real 'you' is not limited.
Why, O pearl, linger you trembling in your shell?
Esteem not yourself mere sugar-cane, but real sugar.
This outward 'you' is foreign to your real 'you';
Cling to your real self, quit this dual self.
(Rūmī, *Spiritual Couplets*, p. 317)

Sufis' guide in their quest for Truth is Love; emotions stir their imagination and without them the 'diver' would not be able to get 'the pearls of wisdom' from the ocean deep. "He in whom the Active Imagination is not at work will never penetrate to the heart of the question" (Ibn 'Arabī, *Futūḥāt*, 2.248; quoted in H. Corbin, *Creative Imagination*, p. 382). Ibn 'Arabī predicted that imagination was born in a loving heart only and that "the science of the heart" was contrary to rational knowledge.

In Sufi symbolism the heart is a receptacle of the Divine Essence and, at the same time, a special organ of mystical comprehension. According to the renowned *ḥadīth qudsī* Allah declared, "Heaven and earth contain Me not, but the heart of my faithful servant contains Me." The heart is like a mirror in which the Divine Light is reflected, but this mirror has to be polished properly that one might see in it God's image. One who has started on the way of the quest for Truth should direct his efforts at this polishing, at achieving moral perfection. When a mystic says that his knowledge is contained in his heart he means knowledge in faith, and every true lover of God seeking to apprehend Him possesses that belief. Man dissatisfied with rational explantions of the eternal secret of the universe frequently turns to belief as a means of liberation from painful ignorance and reaching spiritual balance. But belief brings salvation only on condition of boundless love for the object of belief—the Absolute Being.

Some researchers considered the concept of love to have been "a discovery" of Christianity, first expressed in the Epistles of St. Paul; others found its source in the Song of Songs of the Old Testament. It seems, however, that the roots of the concept go to much greater depth: the idea "He that loveth not knoweth not God" (1 John 4:8) had been clearly enunciated in ancient Hindu religiophilosophical texts, in particular in the "Bhagavadgītā":

> Neither by study of Vedas, nor by penance, nor by charity, nor by ritual can I be seen in this Form (with four arms) as you have seen Me.
>
> Through single-minded devotion, however I can be seen in this Form (with four arms), and known in essence and even entered into, O valiant Arjuna.
>
> Arjuna, he who works for My sake, depends on Me, is devoted to Me, has no attachment, and is free from malice towards all beings, reaches Me.
>
> (11.53–55)

A number of ayats of the Koran indicate that the Truth is apprehended by the heart through love for God. Muhammad Iqbal, in his *Payām-i-mashriq* (p. 288) advises:

> O you who seek the solution of the secret of eternity
> Once your heart's eyes are open the destinies of the
> world are unveiled.

Still it must be confessed that the idea of love for God was only minimally developed in the Koran and Sunna. It was thrown into the shade by the dominant feature of Muslim doctrine: submission, subjection, obedience to the Omnipotent, Omnipresent, and Chastising Ruler. It was in Islamic mysticism that the idea found full scope. The idea of loving God had become central in Sufism and was most expressly manifested in poetry, where God was often associated with a beloved and the poet with a lover:

Let my heart which is a wanderer
In love be a greater wanderer;
Let my body which is a wretched sore
Because of this heart of mine
Be wretched sore, all the more. . . .
I hope sometime to have sight of Thee to the fill,
How long with my eyes at Thy door I have to be waiting
and waiting.
(Amīr Khusrau, *Memorial Volume*, pp. 89, 77)

In other cultures the notion of femininity is used as an allegory for knowing the Eternal. It is enough to recollect the etymology of the word "philosopher," which means literally "the lover of *sophia* (understanding, knowledge, wisdom)." Aristotle and Plato used the term *sophia* to denote knowledge of the essence while in the late Wisdom literature it meant "God's Wisdom," a sort of personal being endowed with "feminine passiveness" (S.S. Averintsev, *Filosofskaya entsiklopedia*, 5:62).

Ibn ʿArabī tried to explain why the contemplation of God (*shahāda* or *mushahāda*) in women "is the most intense and the most perfect" (*Wisdom of the Prophets*, p. 120). It implies a certain polarity of subject and object. Since it is impossible to contemplate God directly, "for God, in his Absolute Essence, is independent of worlds" (ibid.), man selects for contemplation woman as a creature polar to himself and formed from him and after his likeness.Ibn ʿArabī writes: "Woman duplicates man. . . .When man contemplates God in woman, his contemplation rests on that which is passive; if he contemplates Him in himself, seeing that woman comes from man, he contemplates Him in that which is active, and when he contemplates Him alone, without the presence of any form whatsoever issued from Him, his contemplation corresponds to a state of passivity with regard to God, without intermediary" (ibid., pp. 119–20). Such contemplation is the most perfect.

Ibn ʿArabī's explanation does not make explicit the real reasons why the Divine Wisdom is represented as a beloved woman. Nonetheless, Sufis expressed their desire and adoration for the Transcendental, for God, in the easily comprehensible form of man's carnal love for woman.

A Sufi's love is all-absorbing and inexhaustible. It has no bounds because the source of knowledge is unfathomable. The Truth always remains inaccessible, like a beautiful girl passionately loved but ever out of reach.

Sufi poet usually described a mystic as a Madjnūn mad with love. In Rūmī's parable the Caliph asked Layla, "Art thou she by whom Madjnūn was distracted and led astray? Thou art not superior to other fair ones." "Be silent", she replied, "since thou art not Madjnūn." "Whosoever is awake (to the material world) is the more asleep (to the spiritual world); his wakefulness is worse than his sleep." (2:25).

Sufis imagined the process of acquiring knowledge to be akin to intoxication that leads to ecstasy and madness:[4]

> The hand of mine eye gave me love's strong wine to drink,
> when my cup was the face of Her that transcendeth beauty,
> And in my drunkenness, by means of a glance I caused
> my comrades to fancy that it was the quaffing of *their* wine
> that gladdened my inmost soul,
> Although mine eyes made me independent of my cup, and
> my inebriation was derived from her qualities, not from
> my wine;...
> My finding her (in my heart) effacing me, whilst my
> losing her brings me back to myself....
> And my being oblivious (of myself) in Her caused me
> to lose my reason, so that I did not return to myself or
> follow any desire of mine in consequence of my thinking
> (that I existed)....
> (So was I seeking Her within me) until there rose from me
> to mine eye a gleam, and the splendour of my daybreak shone
> forth and my darkness vanished.
> (Ibn al-Fāriḍ, *'Tā'iyya*, pp. 199, 200, 246, 247)

These lines of the Arabian mystical poet Ibn al-Fāriḍ give us a most graceful poetic version of the Sufi concept of knowledge: the Truth is attained in personal experience only, in direct encounter with the object of love, in beholding the intuitively imagined image of the Beloved through mystical consciousness. The call to frenzy is but an allegory; the stupor of intoxication should bring sobriety (though this seems a paradox) that provides freedom from generally accepted logic.

Djalāl al-Dīn Rūmī told in his *Mathnawī* the story of Canaan, a son of Noah, and reverted to it several times. The self-conceited youth would not enter his father's ark but, presuming on his being a good swimmer (that is, being accomplished in mundane intelligence), attempted to save himself at the time of the deluge, unable to see that the ocean is different from a river and cannot be swum over:

> Would that, like a child, he had been ignorant of devices,
> so that, like children, he might have clung to his mother,
> Or that he had not been filled with traditional knowledge,
> (but) had carried away from a saint the knowledge divinely revealed to the heart! (4:350)

The images of mother and father are symbols of human nature in which, the poet believes, deliverance is to be found:

> Sell intelligence and buy bewilderment, intelligence is
> opinion, while bewilderment is (immediate) vision. (Ibid.)

To perceive and comprehend one's own self a person needs special concentration of spiritual and physical energies. Attaining the Truth, though it is considered to be every Sufi's aim, can be achieved only by the few elect. "There are those who know and those who do not. So, God did not want to guide them all" (Ibn 'Arabī, *Wisdom of the Prophets*, p. 43).

The Koran (Sura 6, ayat 39) notes: "Whom God willeth, He leaveth to wander: whom He willeth, He placeth on the way that is straight." The Sacred Book and the Prophet's sayings (Sunna) contain much that is obscure; it is the prerogative of the spiritual elite to comprehend and elucidate it. Ibn 'Arabī wrote:

> All that the prophets brought of sciences is clothed in forms which are accessible to the most ordinary intellectual capacities,

> so that he who does not go to the heart of things stops at this clothing and takes it for what which is the most beautiful, whereas the man of subtle comprehension, the diver who fishes for pearls of Wisdom, knows how to indicate for what reason such or such a Divine Truth is clothed in terrestrial form; he evaluates the robe and the material of which it is made, and knows by that, all that it covers, attaining thus to a science which remains inaccessible to those who do not have knowledge of this order. (Ibid., p. 106)

Such distinction between the spiritual elite who attain to esoteric true knowledge and the common people is characteristic not only of Sufism. It was instituted for a variety of reasons by representatives of many trends in medieval Islam. Sunna taught that "He who puts knowledge before those unprepared for it is like one who puts a necklace of precious stones and pearls and gold on swine." The righteous Calif ʿAlī preached the same: "Tell people only what they understand, so that they will not ascribe falsehoods to God and His Prophet" (F. Rosenthal, *Knowledge Triumphant*, p. 82). The theological precept of distinguishing the elite from the masses realized the intention of excluding common people from participation in the solution of doubtful, perplexing, and controvertible problems, especially those that contradicted rationalist notions, so that there might arise no doubts in the probity of the Muslim doctrine and no sectarian dissensions.

Muslim philosophers who divided society into two 'spiritual classes' were moved by a totally different urge. For al-Fārābī, Ibn Sīnā, Ibn Rushd, and other medieval Muslim thinkers this distinction was a means of delivering philosophy from the heavy press of orthodox religion. Ibn Rushd discriminated three classes of people in relation to their ability to interpret Scripture: the rhetorical class, the overwhelming mass, who are totally incapable of interpretation; people of dialectical interpretation, dialecticians either by nature alone or by nature and habit; and apodictics, the demonstrative class,[5] whose "interpretation achieved through training in the art of philosophy ought not to be expressed to the dialectical class, let alone to the masses. . . .true allegories ought not to be set down in popular books" (Ibn-Rushd, *Harmony*, pp. 67–68).

Sufis assert the existence of both esoteric and exoteric knowledge not only because this allows them to safeguard their personal apprehension of belief free from both dogmatic theology and the intermission of theologians, but also because this proves the impossibility of finding verbal expression for their mystic experience. When a Sufi asserts that his consciousness of inability to attain the Truth is itself consciousness and knowledge, he has in mind not Man's insufficient capacity of perception but the inexpressibility of the Truth perceived. Ibn ʿArabī wrote: "But amongst us there is one who knows (truly), and does not say these words, his knowledge does not imply a powerlessness to know, it implies the inexpressible; it is this latter that has the most perfect consciousness of God" (*Wisdom of the Prophets*, pp. 24–25). Thus Sufis comply fully with the generally accepted principle of mysticism, "silence is the highest wisdom," or as the Chinese sages formulated it, "Those who know do not speak, he who speaks does not know" ("Tao Te Ching" 56).[6]

> As far as the sea it is a journey on horseback: after this
> you (must) have a wooden horse.
> The wooden horse is no good on the dry land: it carries
> exclusively those who voyage on the sea.
> The wooden horse is this (mystical) silence: (this) silence
> gives instruction to the sea-folk.
> Every (such) silent one who wearies you is (really)
> uttering shrieks of love yonde.
> You say, "I wonder why he is silent"; he says (to himself),
> "How strange! Where is his ear?
> I am deafened by the shrieks, (yet) he is unaware (of them)".
> The (apparently) sharp-eared are (in fact) def to this
> (mystical) converse.
>
> (Rūmī, *Mathnawī*, 6:513–14)

For transmitting true knowledge there is only one practical (though not quite effective) way: that of symbols and signs that stimulate imagination. Sufi literature abounds in parables, similies, apologues, allusions, allegories. Most frequent are duplex metaphors: a moth and a candle, a nightingale and a rose—a lover and his Beloved, a Sufi seeking Truth and God-Truth. The moth and the nightingale undergo suffering to achieve unity with the Beloved only through "being burnt in the flames of Love" or stung to death by the rose's lethal thorns. The correlation of Man's self with the cosmic self is denoted by the symbols of a drop of water and the ocean. The act of perceiving Truth is compared to intoxication, with the Sufi a carouser and Truth wine, while the prophet or sheikh is the cupbearer. In order to attain the Turth, to see in all existence nothing but Allāh, one should be capable, first of all, of distinguishing Divine signs and symbols. A common man guided by sensory reason, according to Rūmī, should learn to apply for help to spiritual preceptors, to sages:

> The intelligent man is he who hath the lamp:
> He is the guide and leader of the caravan.
> (*Mathnawī*, 4:393)

There are three kinds of creatures. First, there are the angels, free from mundane passions. "Worship and service and the remembrance of God are their nature." Second, there are the beasts, who are pure lust, having no intelligence[7] to prohibit them. Third, there is Man, who is a compound of intelligence and lust. He is half-angel, half-animal. He is forever in tumult and battle. "He whose intelligence overcomes his lust is higher than the angels; he whose lust overcomes his intelligence is lower than the beasts" (Rūmī, *Discourses*, pp. 89–90).

Men who "have followed their intelligence" become prophets and saints; they are akin to the Universal Mind, or Logos. They have the common morals to obey as soldiers are obedient to their commander (ibid., p. 65), as a blind man follows his guide (*Mathnawī*, 6:485).

> Choose a Pīr, for without a Pīr this journey is exceeding full of woe and affright and danger.

Without an escort you are bewildered (even) on a road
You have travelled many times (before:
Do not, then, travel alone on a way that you have not
seen at all, do not turn your head away from the guide.
(Ibid., 2:160–61).

Who is the *pīr*, the preceptor? It is the 'knower' (*'ārif*), one who "receiving the essential revelation will see his own 'form' in the 'mirror' of God. . .knowing all the while that he sees only his own 'form' by virtue of this Divine mirror," who "adopts the Divine point of view, the object of his knowledge being the same as the object of Divine Knowledge" (Ibn 'Arabī, *Wisdom of the Prophets*, pp. 23, 22). In fact, the 'knower' is much like a Gnostic who is in possession of vision 'in Truth' (as different from the vision 'in the world'), which is attained in the experience of unity with the contemplated. The Gnostic texts from Nag-Hammadi note:

> It is not possible for anyone to see anything of the things that actually exist unless he becomes like them. This is not the way with man in the world: he sees the sun without being a sun, and he sees the heaven and the earth and all other things, but he is not these things. This is quite in keeping with the truth. But you saw something of that place and you became those things. You saw the Spirit, you became Spirit. you saw Christ, you became Christ. You saw (Father, you) shall become Father. So (in this place) you see everything and (you do (not) see) yourself, but (in that place) you do see yourself—and what you see you shall (become). (Codex 2, 3, 44).

The authentic Truth is attained, therefore, both by *'ārifs* and Gnostics who are capable of doing away with the borderlines between the subject and the object, and not only of *recognizing* the Eternal Absolute in their own self but also of *experiencing* the Absolute, of being united with it.

The "essential gifts," the perception of Essence, are granted by Divine revelation or (as emotionalists say) irradiation, emanation of the Divine Light (Ibn 'Arabī, *Wisdom of the Prophets*, p. 23). The immediate knowledge proceeding from God is given only to the Seal of the Prophets (*khātim al-rusul*) and to the Seal of the Saints (*khātim al-awliyā'*), that being the title of Muḥammad. "All prophets, without exception, since Adam. . .imbibed then (their light) in the tabernacle[8] of the Seal of the Prophets" (ibid., p. 27).

Muḥammad, like the Christian Logos, before he was born in bodily form "stayed with God"; "in the Divine Presence," he was the first creature, the first self-determination of the Absolute. Yet there is a difference: in Christianity Jesus was the only, the single manifestation (incarnation) of the Logos;[9] in Sufism the Divine Logos was represented by a long line of prophets, God's messengers (*rasūl*, pl. *rusul*), concluded by Muḥammad, the last *rasūl* according to terrestrial count and the first *rasūl*, from the viewpoint of eternity. All the messengers had been "inspired with Muḥammad's light." They had received their knowledge of the Law in the tabernacle of the Seal of the Sainthood (or of the Saints) (ibid., p. 25), in the inexhaustible source of the Logos. Ibn 'Arabī wrote: "The function of the messenger of God and that of the prophet. . .in so far as it brings about the promulgation of a sacred law ceases, whereas saintliness never ceases; so, the messengers only recieve this knowledge because they are also saints, and solely from the tabernacle of the Seal of Saints" (ibid.).

Contrary to religious doctrine for which Law is uppermost Sufis consider saints superior "with regard to the Knowledge of God" (ibid., p. 26). Of the two hypostases of Muḥammad, the Seal of the Sainthood and the Seal of God's messengers, Sufis consider the first the most important for they esteem Spirit superior to Law. Muḥammad was born once as the Seal of the Prophets, but as the Seal of the Sainthood he is intemporal, the eternally creative spirit manifesting himself in the endless chain of saints.

Sufism prescribes an adept who seeks the Path to choose a preceptor and follow him like a blind man follows his guide. That trend, naturally undermined the position of traditional theologians (*'ulamā'*) and heightened the role of Sufi sheikhs. The practice of Sufi orders shows that sheikhs became masters of unquestioned authority; their disciples (*murids*) absolutely obeyed them as a rule. Still—and it is worthy of note—obedience was not obligatory for all Sufis, but only for the common rank and file. One "possessing his own light," having reached perfection, followed no prescribed rules and standards but the line of behavior he independently chose for himself.

In Sura 18 (ayats 67–81) of the Koran *Khiḍr* is mentioned as a young man instructing Moses and superior to him though Moses' mission was transmitting God's Law to men. *Khiḍr* disclosed to Moses the secret, the mystical truth (*ḥaqīqa*) surpassing the limits of the Law. "I will announce unto thee the interpretation of that thou couldst not bear with patience" (18, 79).

One Muslim tradition calls *Khiḍr* Noah's offspring in the fifth generation; no chronological consideration is possible here, for his meeting Moses would then be quite unaccountable. The definition of *Khiḍr* is so complicated a task that even the compilers of *A Shorter Encyclopaedia of Islam* found it too difficult. In Muslim literature *Khiḍr* is given all sorts of names: prophet, messenger, eternal wanderer, wonderful old man, fulfiller of wishes, eternally living, cupbearer (N. Prigarina, *Poetika*, pp. 39, 80, 82, 192). This multiplicity of designations is due to, it seems, his never appearing as a particular character; in fact, he is not someone distinct from "the seeker of the Truth; but that seeker's "second self."

Ibn 'Arabī told in an autobiographical story how he had had a rather violent discussion with his master (Abu 'l Ḥasan al-Uryāmī) concerning the identity of the person whom the Prophet had favored with his apparition, stood firm in his opinion, and then, somewhat vexed and dissatisfied, took his leave. At a turn in the street a stranger spoke to him affectionately: "Trust your master. It was indeed that person." The young man retraced his steps, meaning to inform his master that he had changed his mind, but on seeing him the sheikh stopped him with these words: "Must Khiḍr appear to you before you trust your master's words?" (quoted in H. Corbin, *Creative Imagination*, p. 63). Ibn 'Arabī happened to meet *Khiḍr* several more times in his life, as he recollected.

Thus *Khiḍr* appears as a mysterious preceptor, a guide showing the true way: "He leads each disciple to his own theophany, the theophany of which he persaonlly is the witness because that theophany corresponds to his 'inner heaven', to the form of his own being, to his eternal individuality. . .which, in Ibn ʿArabī's words, is that one of the Divine Names which is invested in him" (ibid., p. 61).

In the exoteric sphere *Khiḍr* appears as a master, a preceptor, as one of scores of thousands of saints, or even as one of the prophets (*nabī*). In the esoteric aspect this preceptor is not a phantom, but the true human self.

It is of importance that the name "Khiḍre," a mangled form of Khāḍīr, means "the Verdant One" (ibid., p. 56). Since green is the color of Islam it might signify that the term "The Verdant One" reflects the idea of Man's close connection with the Divine, *Khiḍr* being the Divine self of every Man-microcosm. It was not by chance that Muhammad Iqbal asked himself, "What is the message of *Khiḍr* and gave the answer, "the command of the cosmos" (N. Prigarina, *Poetika*, p. 92).

Ibadat Barelwi, a Pakistan critic, has remarked in his analysis of M. Iqbal's poem "Khiḍr-i ra" that in the poet's dialogue with Khiḍr the voices of the two interlocutors coalesce, so that the poem may be considered monological. The coalescence seems to corroborate the idea that *Khiḍr* is Man's 'inner voice,' a pure voice unsullied by mundane and carnal passions. Another evidence is the comparison of *Khiḍr* with a cupbearer who is a symbol of true (real) knowledge in Sufi parlance.

The disguising and ensconcing of the image of *Khiḍr* is not a matter of chance. It corresponds to the general style of Muslim mystics' doctrine expounded habitually in a complicated manner incomprenensible to the uninitiated.

> Khusrau's ghazals are not intelligible to every one,
> Only a lover's heart may judge of them, none else.
> (Amīr Khusrau, *Memorial Volume*, p. 7)

Sufis regarded skeptically the belief forced upon Man externally. To it they counterposed the faith born in the internal, individual experience of a "loving heart." The Sufian *ma ʿrifa* denoted knowledge gained in personal experience, mystically revealed. The idea that "each does not know of God except that which he infers from himself" (Ibn ʿArabī, *Wisdom of the Prophets*, p. 13) is a most clear and ample expression of the Sufi concept of knowledge.

Sufis asserted that "God is unknowable." Al-Ḥallādj exclaimed, "L'homme ne sait meme pas, devant un poil de son corps, comment il a ete plante, noir ou blanc; comment connaitrait-il Celui qui fait exister les choses?" ("Man knows nothing even about a hair on his own body, how it has grown, why it is black of blonde; how could he know The One who made everything exist? [quoted in L. Massignon, *La passion*, p. 889]). The famous mystic proved (in chapter 11 of his treatise *Kitāb aṭ-ṭawāsīn*) how groundless were the arguments intended to show the comprehensibility of the Absolute. He underlined the fallacy of such claims as, "Je Le connais, parce que j' existe" (I know Him because I exist"), or "Je Le connais par Son Nom" (I know Him by His Name"), or "Je Le connais par Son oeuvre" (I know Him by His creation"), or "Je Le connais par Ses paires d'attributs antithetiques" (I know Him by His pairs of antithetical attributes") (ibid., pp. 887–89). Having rejected vain pretences to attainment of wisdom, al-Hallādj concludes, "La Sagesse se tient a l'ecart des choses existentiels. . . . Il n'y a pas de route qui y accede. Ses significations sont claires: il n'y pas de preuve qui les etablisse. Les sens ne La percoivent pas, les adjectifs qu'emploient les hommes ne L'atteignent pas" ("Wisdom keeps away from creaturely things. . . .There is no way that leads to Her. Her significations are clear—there are no proofs to establish them. Senses do not perceive Her, the attributes used by men cannot be applied to Her" [ibid., p. 891]).

While Islamic theologians' skepticism concerning the possibility of getting knowledge of God and providence[10] signified the senselessness of attempts at attaining the Truth and the necessity of compliance with the letter of the Sacred Book and with the legal prescriptions of Islam, Sufi skepticism contained something quite different. For a mystic the impossibility of perfect realization of the Absolute meant not submission to the dogma and blind acceptance of it but incessant striving to achieve maximum realization. Al-Ghazālī wrote: "The incapacity of complete comprehension is comprehension; glory be to Him who has created for men the way of comprehending Him only by their incapacity of comprehending Him" (*Voskresenie*, p. 248). Sufi notions about the incomprehensibleness of the Absolute did not close the ways of cognition; on the contrary, it asserted the infinity of the process of cognition, the necessity of perpetual quest for Truth. Craving for true hidden gnosis was accounted for by feelings worthy of a true believer and lover of God. Al-Ghazālī thus described it: "If he turns his gaze beyond the veil of the hidden to the summit of beauty conscious of his incapacity to perceive the essence of the magnificance, and his heart strains in calling for it, thrills, and trembles before it, that state of anxiety is called anguish. It is anguish after the hidden" (ibid., p. 251). "Anguish after the hidden" is a cryptic Sufi formula denoting "constant seeking for Truth."[11] That unquenchable thirst for knowledge, that anguish after the hidden, contained an immense positive charge of Sufism that attracted floundering minds and souls.

3

The Path of Perfection

In prayer
I will never dissemble,
Never will I beg
At any door save the door of Knowledge,
I am the king of all I survey
I enjoy freedom from want—
Never will I eschew my love for the tavern.
Sarmad Shaheed

Alongside Man's determination to abide by enunciated norms there exists (or, rather, runs counter to it)—as evidenced by the history of the spiritual culture of most peoples—a tendency to regulate conduct in accordance with an internal, personal conception of good and evil.

To illustrate this we can turn to the history of ancient China and compare the image of the Perfect Man in Taoism and Confucianism. In Confucianism the perfect man (*chün-tzu*) is the ideal of a citizen. Confucius said that humanity consisted in learning to master oneself and restoring the observance of righteousness (*li*). He strove to preserve 'the general order' by directing *chün-tzu* to fulfill steadily their social duty. The ancient book *Lun-yü* (*Analects*) taught that private desires were to be suppressed for the sake of common interests and that dutiful behavior meant vanquishing personal propensity and returning to the rules of *li*, that is, to regular norms of social morality.

Taoism also calls for suppression of the ego but the real man (*chi jen*) is believed to be in perfect conformity with 'the omnipotent and omnipresent' absolute One—Tao. Man's main aim is returning to Tao, to the Unity, to nature by means of forsaking and forgetting the personal (the superficial, the artificial) and rejecting the individual self. In a parable of Chuang Tzu[1] we read that a man "after he had put life outside himself, was able to achieve the brightness of dawn, and when he had achieved the brightness of dawn, he could see his own aloneness. After he had managed to see his own aloneness, he could do away with past and present, and after he had done away with past and present, he was able to enter where there is no life and no death" (*Complete Works*, p. 83).

Since Tao is essentially immanent to the universe, 'overcoming self' means perfecting oneself through discarding the superfluous, unreal self so that the real self might be revealed. *Chi jen* is in harmony with Tao, that is, with his own true nature.

Muslim culture contains a rather similar parallelism of two trends in regulating Man's behavior: one directed mainly at following the external rules and norms sanctioned by society, the other oriented internally, in one's own self-perceived principles of the Absolute One. The first trend is represented by the Muslim creed in its various forms, the second by Muslim mysticism.

The adepts of Sufism believed that perfect conduct transcended the boundaries of legalized religious doctrine, sometimes even ignoring or denying them. The formula "There is no God save Allah and Muḥammad is His Prophet" was accepted by Sufis but their treatment of it was markedly distinct from the codified notion: to the institutionalized Islamic monotheism Sufis opposed an intrinsically pantheistic idea of God and the created world, an idea that legalist theologians disclaimed as a most pernicious one.[2]

Sufis accepted Muḥammad's prophethood; however, they tended to see in him not only 'God's Messenger' but some cosmic force as well, a life-giving spirit of the Absolute Essence itself, 'the Reality of Muḥammad' (*al-haqīqa al-Muḥammadiyyah*). Ibn ʿArabī and his followers used to refer to the *ḥadīth* "I was a prophet when Adam was still between water and clay" (*Wisdom of the*

Prophets, p. 27) and assert that though Muḥammad was the last of prophets, 'the Seal of the Messengers' in temporal chronology, he was notwithstanding the eternally emanating Divine Light (*nūr*). Rūmī makes Muḥammad speak of "The Soul of the World" in this way:

I have circled a while with the nine Fathers in each Heaven
[nine planets in nine celestial spheres],
For years I have revolved with the stars in their signs.
I was invisible a while, I was dwelling with Him.
I was in the kingdom of 'or nearer', I saw what I have seen.
I receive my nourishment from God, as a child in the womb;
Man is born once, I have been born many times.
(*Dīwān*, p. 182)

The *wudjūdiyya* diverge from the traditional interpretation of Muḥammad's prophecy and characterize his essence and functional role according to their basic idea of the Unity of Being (*wahḍat al-wudjūd*). For them Muḥammad the Prophet is a particular (the most perfect, to be sure) manifestation of the eternally creative, life-giving power of the Absolute, of the Light whose emanation is the world.

Mystics who repudiated mediators and insisted on direct communion between God and Man admitted the necessity of the second prescription of Islam, that of daily prayers. Still, there was a difference: while for a common Muslim five prayers a day provide 'a key to paradise,' for a Sufi praying was not so flagrantly pragmatic; it was his soul's cry of lament evoked by suffering because of his separation from and striving eagerly to be united with the Beloved (God).

My heart has of the world grown weary, and all that it can lend:
The shrine of my affection holds in Being but my friend.
If e'er for me thy love's sweet garden a fragrant breath exhale,
My heart, expansive in its joy, shall bird-like burst its veil—
I find the arch of the *Miḥrāb* but in an eyebrow's bow.
(Ḥāfiẓ, *Selections*, p. 96)

Not all Sufis admit the urgency of regular prayer; some prefer to address God in silence and secret. This attitude resembles many Christian mystics' conception of prayer. Meister Eckhart, for one, was certain of the greater import of silence. It is in peace and quiet "that God can speak and act in him . . . , the very best and utmost of attainment in this life is to remain still and let God act and speak in thee" (F. C. Happold, *Mysticism*, p. 277).

Praying should not amount to supplication. Entreating for benefits is immoral from the Sufi view; it is a shameful low bargaining ("I shall praise You and You will requite me for it") In fact, as Ibn ʿArabī wrote, "God will give him (who asks Him) nothing that does not result from this essence (al-*ʿayn*), that he is himself in his permanent principal state [the suppliant's human nature]" (*Wisdom of the Prophets*, p. 22). The Sufis who acknowledged the value of praying did not fail to remark that for a common Muslim it was a duty enjoined by the Sharīʿa while for a mystic it was the fulfillment of the desire "to have secret communion with God." God, the interlocutor, proved to be in fact the believer's second self and the prayer resolved itself into an internal dialogue. "In praising that which he believes, the believer praises his own soul" (ibid., p. 132).

There were certain audacious quietists who protested openly against the ritual of regular praying, which they considered useless: "What use has the drowning person for shouting? Only that he is the sooner drowned" (A. Schimmel, *Mystical Dimensions*, p. 156). Those men were staunch enough to declare plainly that they did not observe that paramount Islamic ritual. Thus ʿAbd Allāh Ibn Mubārak said, "It is about fifty years since I have prayed or wished anyone to pray for me" (ibid., p. 156). Evidently, the defiant spirits were not scarce since al-Ghazālī found it necessary to rebuke them in a special chapter of his treatise *Revival of the Religious Sciences*, where he insisted that "prayer is God's commandment" (*Voskresenie*, p. 258).

Most of the Sufis, however, admitted outwardly the necessity of regular prayer though they preferred the 'free' prayer (*du ʿā*') and especially the 'recollection' of God's name (*dhikr*). *Dhikr* was considered mystics' own particular form of adoration, grounded as it was upon a number of Koranic ayats, such as "O ye who believe! celebrate the praises of God, and do this often" (Sura 33, 41), or "Those who believe, and whose hearts find satisfaction in the remembrance of God: for without doubt in the remembrance of God do hearts find satisfaction" (Sura 13, 28).

The propriety of considering *dhikr* "the main means of attaining God's nearness"[3] was upheld by numerous *ḥadīths* like Muḥammad's "He who recollects God among the negligent is like a fighter in the midst of those who flee, like a green tree in the midst of dry trees." The Prophet was asked what action was most virtuous. He answered, "That you should be dying and your tongue should recollect Allah the Mighty, the Omnipotent." The Prophet said, "Praising Allah. . . in the morning and in the evening is better than erecting mosques in Allah's name or generous sacrifice of money."[4]

Islamic mysticism distinguishes two kinds of *dhikr*: pronouncing the name of Allah aloud and doing it silently. In the first case Sufis practiced certain forms of breath control, a method of concentration that brought them into an ecstatic state. Music and rhythmical movement (whirling dances of dervishes of the Mawlawīyya order, for example) also helped Sufis reach ecstasy. The orthodox Muslims greatly depreciated listening to music and objected to infatuation with dancing; the official religion denounced *samā'* (listening to music and dancing movement) as 'false revelry' inconsistent with true belief (al-Ghazālī, *Voskresenie*, p. 130).

In spite of all indictments and proscriptions music was generally part of Sufi rites. in the second part of the ninth century special houses (*sam*ā' khānas) appeared in which Sufis could listen to music; mention of them is found in early Sufi literature (for instance, in al-Ḥallādj's writings). As Ye. E. Bertels notes, the term *samā'* had a wide meaning and could denote "everything listened to, from recitation or reading of texts to music (instrumental and vocal)" (*Sufism*, p. 58); in fact, it also connoted listening together to chanting of verses. Contending against the charges of theologians Sufis used to present numerous proofs of permissibility and, moreover, desirability or *samā'* in their treatises. Al-Ghazālī devoted an entire chapter of his *Revival of the Religious Sciences* to the "Results and Rules of listening to music": "Listening to Music and Poetry helps purify the heart and the purification of the heart leads to revelation" (*Voskresenie*, p. 108); "When hearts are inflamed with love for Allah an unfamiliar *beyt* (a distich chanted) excites in them what the recitation of Quran might not do" (ibid., p. 123). Still, al-Ghazālī, faithfully adhering to his intention of "reconciling" Sufism with the orthodox doctrine of Islam, suggested a compromise. Music and dancing should be forbidden to the majority of people, in whom these activities stir up "a passion for the corrupt world" and "ignominious proclivities" (ibid., p. 131). *Samā'* is desirable for the elect, "ruled by love for Allah the Allmighty", in whom listening arouses only "laudable emotions" (ibid., p. 131).

Al-Ghazālī's ratiocination about the admissibility and usefulness of *samā'* for true *murids* was developed more fully in the works of representatives of the Chishtī order. It should be noted, however, that there were antagonists of *samā'* among Sufis themselves. Thus, members of the Naqshbandīyya order rejected it altogether. The Mawlawīyya (Mevlevīyya) order, on the contrary, backed *samā'* and rhythmical dancing, unreservedly. Djalāl al-Dīn Rūmī, the spiritual father of the order, compared the whirling movement of the dervishes to workers treading on grapes, an act that brought the "spiritual wine" into existence and created the illusion of union with god (A. Schimmel, *Mystical Dimensions*, pp. 183–84).

Many of the Sufis preferred the silent *dhikr*, quoting the Prophet's word: "You do not call upon a Death one and not an Absent one, but you call upon a Hearing one who is with you wherever you are!" Pronouncing God's name aloud and praising Him vociferously would disturb the mediation of other believers. If the Almighty was both transcendent and immanent at the same time, Man's prayer should be interiorized.

> Both of us are a single worshipper who, in respect
> of the united state, bows himself to his own essence
> in every act of bowing.

None prayed to me but myself, nor did I pray to anyone
but myself in the performance of every genuflexion.
(Ibn-Fārid, Ta'iyyatu'l Kubra, verses 153–54;
quoted in R. A. Nicholson, *Islamic Mysticism*, p. 214)

Sufi attitude to *ḥadjdj* (pilgrimage to Mecca) was no less seditionary from the point of view of the Muslim traditional religion. Though many Sufis visited the sacred places several times, still there were those among them who did not consider Ka'ba "the true seat of the Divine spirit" since they believed that the real tabernacle was the faithful worshiper's heart. The Turkish mystic Yūnus Emre wrote: "When you seek God, seek Him in your heart—He is not in Jerusalem, nor in Mecca, nor in the ḥadjdj" (quoted in A. Schimmel, *Mystical Dimensions*, p. 106). In other words, Sufis counterpoised to pilgrimage, an external show of piety, an internal 'pilgrimage' into the depth of one's own consciousness or soul, it being a real 'divine treasure.' Still most dervishes performed pilgrimages to the tombs of Sufi preceptors that were sacred places for mystics. The orthodox Islam treated such pilgrimages as recusancy, even idolatry.

As regards fasting in the month of *Ramaḍān* and *zakāt* (payment of the tax for succoring the poor), Sufis held extreme views. They considered fasting a most essential condition of their mystical practice; the principle of their daily conduct was "little food, little sleep, little talk." The month of fast in *Ramaḍān* did not seem sufficient to them and they often practiced the so-called *ṣaum dā'ūdī*, eating one day and fasting the next throughout the year. Early Sufis praised hunger in general, asserting that abstaining from food "could transform the darkness of the heart into light" and make way for spiritual food granted by God. Later Sufi orders relinquished this practice of early ascetics. Naqshbandīyya, for example, asserted that "the people who truly fast are those who keep their minds free from the food of satanic suggestions and so do not allow any impure thoughts to enter their hearts" (ibid., p. 117).

Zakāt was altogether out of place for members of many orders, such as Chishtī, whose ideal was permanent poverty and subsisting on alms only. They referred to the tradition of Muḥammad, claiming, "Poverty is my pride," and considered indifference to mundane goods a necessary condition for pursuing the Path. "He who does not possess *faqr* is not a Sufi" (*Muslim Philosophy*, Vol. 1, p. 357). It is not by chance that the word *faqīr* (meaning "poor") is identified with the name "Sufi" in Muslim countries.

Observance of *Sharīʿa* injunctions is obligatory for adepts in the initial stage of the path to perfection. But mystics could not be satisfied with the legalistic code of behavior as they strove to something greater than righteousness as admitted by orthodox canons. They hoped to attain unity with the Absolute by apprehending their own self and the Divine self in it. They considered *Sharīʿa* the law of the phenomenal world, of the visible, while in order to enter the 'secret world' one had to pass along the more difficult path of *ṭarīqa*, followed by the Perfect Man (or Universal Man, *al-insān al-kāmil*). According to Ibn ʿArabī all the universals are manifested in the Perfect Man who integrates symbolically all being, who is "one single essential reality (*ḥaqīqa*) which assumes all the relations and associations" (*Wisdom of the Prophets*, pp. 28–29). Djalāl al-Dīn Rūmī also asserted that God's gifts were first showered on Muḥammad, the Perfect Man, and then "distributed from him to other men" (*Discourses*, p. 232).

It should be noted, though, that Ibn ʿArabī's Perfect Man was assigned mainly (and probably, solely) the *metaphysical* function of solving the problem of the unique and multiple, of the general and the particular, of essence and phenomenon, while later Sufis thought of *al-insān al-kāmil* primarily as integrating *religious* functions, acting as the intermediary between God and Man.

The level of *al-insān al-kāmil* can be attained by prophets as well as by saints (*al-walī* means "near," and in the Sufi context, "near to God"), who make a sort of popular variety of the Perfect Man. Such are those who happen to be akin to the Universal Reason or Logos. The truly Divine is concentrated in their hearts. Rūmī elucidated the standpoint in a manner very distant from the orthodox style of thinking:

That (mosque) is phenomenal, this (heart) is real, O asses!
The (true) mosque is naught but the hearts of the (spiritual) captains.
The mosque that is the inward (consciousness)of the saints is the place of worship for all: God is there.
(*Mathnawī*, 1:383)

Compliance with both metaphysical and religious definitions of *al-insān al-kāmil* allowed the formation of the principles of moral perfection in accordance with the adept's intellectual level. The majority of adherents to Sufism, plain and generally illiterate folk, followed the guidance and example of *walī*, the master or preceptor. His life and conduct were a model to imitate and to follow, And blind and often thoughtless imitation prospered, so that an adept might become a tool in the hands of deceitful and imperious men who knew how to force the weak and inexperienced to submit to their will.

At the same time, the metaphysical interpretation of *al-insān al-kāmil* contained significant humanitarian potential. It was supposed that the indicator of good and evil should be Man himself, capable of perfection on the path of learning to know himself and to become conscious of his true self.

Ibn al-Fāriḍ, assured as he was that the final aim and meaning of the way to reveal the Absolute in his own self, wrote:

But when I cleared the film from me, I saw myself restored to consciousness, and mine eye was refreshed by the (Divine) Essence. . . .
Therefore mortify thyself that thou mayst behold in thee and from thee a peace beyond what I have described—a peace born of a feeling of calm.
After my self-mortification I saw that he who brought me to behold and led me to my (real) self was I; nay, that I was my own example,
And that my standing (at 'Arafāt) was a standing before myself; nay, that my turning (towards the Ka 'ba) was towards myself. Even so my prayer was to myself and my Ka 'ba from myself.
(Quoted in R. A. Nicholson, *Islamic Mysticism*, p. 221–222)

The concept of Perfect Man, based on the notion of Man as a tabernacle of Divine and the possibility of Man's returning to his true self through unity with God, led to the logical conclusion that God's Essence was immanent to Man's and that was incompatible with the traditional thesis of God's absolute transcendence. The individual's being able to attain the level of *al-insān al-kāmil* carried a challenge to the widely accepted Muslim tenet of fatalism:

> It is known that your slave cannot live without you,
> not a single day,
> Still he longs to exert himself and live in accordance
> with his own will.
> (Hosrov Dehlevi, *Izbrannoye*, p. 19)

The Muslim solution to the problem of the freedom of the will has never been homologous. Neither the Koran nor the Sunna provides a single invariant answer. Still, Islam's assertion of God's omnipotence, the Islamic principle of predestination, and the allegation of the "finality" of Muḥammad's prophecy moved Marx to remark that "Mohammedanism centers upon fatalism" ("War Question," 12:408). A number of ayats in the Koran (Sura 6, 39, 125, 134; Sura 7, 188; Sura 10, 100; Sura 16, 9; Sura 76, 3) deal with the foreordination of Man's fate and his conduct, and yet some of its verses seem to express a disclaimer of blind fatalism.

As early as the time of the first *caliphs* there arose disputes and contentions among the Muslims concerning predestination. The notion's inherent contradiction consisted in its being incompatible with the principle of Man's responsibility for his actions. How could Man be responsible for actions that did not emanate from him but had been preordained by God primordially?[5] How could the conception of Allah the Omnipotent be harmonized with His image of infinite goodness? If God is omnipotent, good and evil exist because He has willed it, and that means He is not absolutely good. If He is absolutely good and evil proceeds from without, that means He is not omnipotent and does not determine men's fates.[6]

In the first two centuries of Islam absolute fatalism had been called into question by Murdji'a and Ḳadariyya. Mu'tazila propagted widely the idea of free will. Muslim mystics were constantly preoccupied with these problems and treated them in disaccord with flagrant fatalism. Admitting complete predetermination of men's actions would make entering the path of perfection senseless, and that was Sufis' aim and purpose, the subject of their exhortations, and the very foundation of their doctrine and practice. Hence arose the intention of combining God's omnipotence and Man's free will.

According to Ibn ʿArabī omnipotence means that "the giver is always God, in the sense that it is He the treasurer of all possibilities" (*Wisdom of the Prophets*, p. 28). The Great Sheikh, nevertheless did not acknowledge necessity only and exclude possiblity. He disparaged as "intellectually feeble" certain thinkers who "have gone so far as to deny the possibility as such and to accept (as logical and ontological categories) only the absolute necessity" (ibid., p. 31). Ibn ʿArabī founds his admission of Man's free will on his certitude that Man is but "a receptacle" of possibility granted to him by God which he must and is able to realize by himself: "From God comes only the effusion of the Being on thee (who art only pure possibility) whereas thine own judgment (*al-ḥukm*) comes from thee. Then, praise only thyself and blame only thyself" (ibid., p. 44).

The theme of free will found vivid and picturesque exposition in poetry of Djalāl al-Dīn Rūmī. The Sufi poet openly denounces fatalism, regarding adherence to it as a vice not just a weakness. One of his parables contains the lion's conversation with other animals. The lion, personifying wisdom, instructs animals that are before him, explaining that God's omnipotence does not limit their independent choices and actions but, on the contrary, presupposes them, and pronouncing exertion to be superior to trust in God.

> Yes, said the Lion, but the Lord of his servants set a ladder
> before our feet.
> Step by step must we climb towards the roof: to be a
> necessitarian here is (to indulge in) foolish hopes.
> You have feet: why do you make yourself out to be lame?
> You have hands: why do you conceal the fingers?

When the master put a spade in the slave's hand, his object was made known to him (the slave) without (a word falling from his) tongue.
Hand and spade alike are His (God's) implicit signs; (our powers of) thinking upon the end are His explicit declarations.
When you take his signs to heart, you will devote your life to fulfilling that indication (of His Will). . . .
Thanksgiving for the power (of acting freely) increases your power, necessitarianism takes the (Divine) gift (of free will) out of your hand;
Your necessitarianism is (like) sleeping in the road: do not sleep! Sleep not, until you see the gate and the threshold! . . .
If you are putting trust in God, put trust (in Him) as regards (your) work: sow (the seed), then rely upon the Almighty!

(*Mathnawī*, 2:52–53)

Thus freedom of will is qualified as God's mercy. Why does the Almighty of His own will limit His might? What is the sense of that? The point is to submit Man to a test.

Put a sword in his hand; pull him away from weakness (incapacity to choose), so that he may become (either) a holy warrior or a brigand.
Because we have honoured Man by (the gift of) free will: half (of him) is honey-bee, half is snake.

(Ibid., 4:185)

Why should God test Man? Could not He endow Man with virtues only? That is what a Sufi asked the judge (*qāḍī*) in Rūmī's *Mathnawī* and got for an answer the poet's favorite argument: chastity is worth nothing unless it be tempted by lust:

How could there be steadfast and sincere and bountiful men without a brigand and an accursed Devil,
Rustam and Hamsa and a (cowardly) catamite would be (all) one; knowledge and wisdom be annulled and utterly demolished.

> Knowledge and wisdom exist for the purpose of (distinguishing between) the right path and the wrong paths; when all (paths) are the right path, knowledge and wisdom are void of meaning.
>
> (Ibid., 6:356)

Still, the main point is not testing Man so that his real worth might be tried and evidenced. The evil and the good are needed to demonstrate the universal scope of the Absolute Being. God is all, and that means, as Ibn ʿArabī concludes, that "He manifests Himself even in the qualities of imperfection and in the qualities deserving blame" (*Wisdom of the Prophets*, p. 40). Muslim mystics accepted the Islamic principle of God's absolute goodness; still they were not inclined to consider the evil an exclusively subjective category.[7] This position seems double-faced in its attempt to reconcile the objectivist and the subjectivist approaches. Sufism, being a mystical trend within a monotheistic religion and contrary to dualistic doctrines, could not accept the ideas of primordial existence of two principles, a good and an evil one. (In Zoroastrianism, for example, the diety Ariman embodied the evil and another diety, Ahuramazdu, personified the good—and, respectively, the armies of light and darkness.) Sufis were conscious, nonetheless, of the vulnerability of the thesis about absolute subjectivity of the category of evil. They possessed a dialectic perception of good and evil as manifestations of God's objective Reality.

> Since eternity it was the will and decree of God, the Forgiver, to reveal and manifest Himself,
> (This involves contrariety, for) nothing can be shown without a contrary to that incomparable King.
> Therefore . . .
> He made two banners, white and black: one (was) Adam, the other (was) the Iblīs (Devil) of the way (to Him).
> Between these two mighty camps (there was) combat and strife, and there came to pass what came to pass.
>
> (Rūmī, *Mathnawī*, 6:378)

In this case Muslim mystics follow the dialectic trend in the historiophilosophic development of the problem of good and evil. The idea that God in order "to be known" manifests Himself in contrasting forms, since the dazzling Divine Light needs opposing darkness to be contemplated, is consonant with the views of Neo-Platonists, who affirmed that vitiation of things cannot be discussed unless there are things that can be vitiated, nor can evil be spoken of unless there is good. Striking analogies appear not only of ideas but of images and metaphors as well. Rūmī's poetical assimilation of good and evil to rival armies engaged in warfare is reminiscent of Tertullian's "God's camp" and "devil's camp."

Good and evil appear as objective manifestations of twin Divine attributes: mercy and revenge. They are the results of Almighty's wish to manifest Himself, so they are determined in a certain sense. But to finish the enquiry here would mean acknowledging good and evil's essential presence in the world and, hence, the uselessness of attempts to vanquish evil. If so, nothing would remain but quietism, a complete submission to God-ordained fate, reconciliation with evil, negation of high ideals, and efforts to achieve personal perfection and social progress. Sufis were conscious of such prospects and endeavored to expound that though good and evil existed objectively Man was free to make his choice. It was a pity he frequently preferred the evil.

In Rūmī's *Mathnawī* (4:349) Iblīs (the Satan) complains that God has disgraced him:

> The colour is Thy colour: Thou art my dyer; Thou art the origin of my sin and bane and brand.

Rūmī disproves Iblīs, and thus all others who having sinned put the blame of God:

> How long will you leap up the tree of necessitarianism and lay your free will aside?. . . .
> How should there be compulsion when you are trailing your skirt (sweeping along) into sin with such complacence?

Does anyone under compulsion walk so complacently?
Does anyone, having lost his way, go dancing (gleefully) like that?

(*Mathnawī*, 4:349)

Muslim mystics believed, in accordance with the Koranic version of the story (7, 10–24), that the fall of Adam, forefather of mankind, had taken place because of Satan's seduction. But they saw, characteristically, in Adam's fall evil begetting good, for if Adam had not sinned he would not have been banished from Paradise and could not have become sovereign of everything on the earth. Sufis were inclined to interpret the meaning of Adam's seduction and the role of Satan, his seducer, in a manner different from that of the Koran and the Bible. They did not consider Satan God's enemy but His auxiliary in testing Man. This allows some researchers to arrive at the conclusion that Sufism contained a tendency of indemnifying Satan.

Such a tendency, to be sure, may be traced in the views of a number of prominent representatives of Islamic mysticism. Manṣūr al-Ḥallādj, ʿAṭṭār, and others. The pathos of al-Ḥallādj's concept of Iblīs consists, indeed, in singing praise to the "feat" of Satan, represented as a martyr who suffered for his monotheism. According to Ḥallādj, Iblīs was at first an angel, the most righteous among angels. "Il n'y avait pas, parmi les habitants du ciel, de monothèiste (muwaḥḥid) comparable a Satan: l'Essence lui apparut dans toute sa purete" ("There was among the inhabitants of heaven no monotheist (*muwaḥḥid*) to be compared with Satan: the Essential Being appeared to him in all the purity" [L. Massignon, *La passion*, p. 868]). The fall of Iblīs occurred when God demanded him to prostrate himself before Adam and Iblīs retorted, "Pas devant un autre (que Toi)!. . .Je renie (Ton ordre). . ., c'est pour T'affirmer Saint! . . .Qu'est ce qu'Adam? Rien, sans Toi!" ("Not before another (but Thou)!. . .My rebillion means to declare Thee Holy!. . .What is Adam? He is nothing without Thou! [ibid., p. 869]).

Al-Ḥallādj acclaimed, in fact, the act of disobedience of Iblīs: "Satan est plus ferré qu'eux sur l'adoration, il est plus proche qu'eux de l'Etre, il a sacrifié davantage au zèle de Le servir, il a tenu plus qu'eux son sermon, il s'est approché plus qu'eux de l'Adoré" ("Satan knows more about adoration than they [righteous Muslim theologians] and he is nearer than they are to the Being, for he sacrificed more [choosing to forsake his place among angels] in his zeal of serving Him, and was more true to his sermon, and approached the Beloved nearer than they ever did [ibid., p. 876]).

Why did God damn Iblīs and deprive him of angelic appearance? Al-Ḥallādj asserted, first, that it was only the outside of Satan that had been changed, not his inner quality: "La Sagesse acquise persiste, telle qu'elle était au debut, même l'individu (qui la reçue) se trouve déformé" ("The acquired wisdom remains such as it was at first even if the possessor of it gets deformed" [ibid.]). Second, Satan's "deformation" is not a mark of God's punishment but rather an indication of his being elected: "Il m'a ecarte loin des autres vu mon zèle (pour Lui seul). . . . Il m'a délaissé parce qu'il S'etait découvert à moi. Il m'a mis à nu, parce qu'il m'avait fait inhérent (à Sa prescience), Il m'a fait inhérent (a Sa prescience) parce qu'il m'avait differencié" ("He put me off [Ibliīs declared] because of my zeal [for Him and no one else]. . . . He kept me aloof because He had revealed Himself to me. He had abandoned me because He had imparted to me [His prescience]. He had imparted [His prescience] to me because He had distinguished me [from others]" [ibid.]).

Satan's being elect finds expression in the duality of his role. At first he was called to preach to angels in heaven and exert them to monotheism (*tawḥīd*); later he was charged with provoking men on earth to bad actions so that they might be tested (ibid., p. 873). Thus, Satan's 'sin' as well as the evil he planted on earth occurred according to God's will. "Si Tu m'as empeché de me prosterner (devant Adam), Toi-m̂eme en as été cause" ("If Thou hinderedst me from prostrating me [before Adam], Thyself wert the cause of it" [Iblīs impeache God]" [ibid., p. 874]).

Farīd al-Dīn ʿAṭṭār (d. 1220), like Manṣūr al-Ḥallādj, envisaged Iblīs as the perfect monotheist and 'lover' (true believer) who accepted God's curse as an honor, for "to be cursed by Thee, is a thousand times dearer to me than to turn my head away from

Thee to anything else" (quoted in A. Schimmel, *Mystical Dimensions*, p. 195). Disobedience is qualified as an act of free will necessary for the choice in favor of good.

A romantic visualization of Satan as part of the eternal power was continued in the poetry of Muhammad Iqbal in the twentieth century.

Rehabilitation of Satan, to be sure, was not the only peculiar trend within Sufism. Many mystics treated Iblīs' refusal to prostrate himself before Adam as a symbol of general disobedience in the phenomenal world, as an act resulting from ignorance ('being one-eyed'). Rūmī repeatedly asserted that Iblīs "is a representation of one-eyed intellectualism" unable to see that Man was created after God's likeness and the Divine spirit breathed into him.[8] But those Sufis who, like Rūmī, were not inclined to a romantic representation of Satan still asserted free will and, hence, Man's responsibility for his actions. They believed that both good and evil came from God but Man could and had to make his choice of them freely.

Rūmī compared God's gift, the possibility of free choice, with the capital (*sarmaya*) that brings profit and enumeration to the owner who knows how to employ it, while one who holds it and does not know how to use it or misuses it will be punished on Doomsday.

> In the world this praise and "well done!" and "bravo!" are
> (bestowed) in virtue of free will and watchful attention. . . .
> The power (of free action) is thy profit-earning capital.
> Mark, watch over the moment of power and observe (it well)!
>
> (*Mathwanī*, 4:85)

Freedom of will, one of the 'damned questions' of philosophy, is a problem Hegel described as "unbestimmt, vieldeutig, der grössten Missverständnisse fähig" ("undeterminate, polysemantic, liable to greatest misunderstandings" [*Werke*, Bd. 7, S. 374]). The freedom of the will may also be considered as a category closely joined to that of knowledge. Freedom of the will then means nothing but the capacity to make decisions with knowledge of the subject. In this sense freedom, in Sufis' worldview, is relatively indeterminate, independent of traditional knowledge.

Thus says Ḥāfiẓ in one of his ghazals:

> Last night our elder set forth for the tavern out of the mosque.
> Friends of the mystic way, henceforward what can we do?
> Let us also become fellow-drinkers in the Magian inn, for so ran the writ of our destiny on the primal day of the world.
> If reason knew how happy the heart is in his tresses' bond,
> The men of reason too would become mad to wear our chain.
> The shaft of our sigh surpasses heaven: Hafiz, be silent!
> Have compassion upon your soul: beware of our shaft.
>
> (Quoted in A. J. Arberry, *Classical Persion Literature*, p. 326)

Sufism cursed blind imitation and repetition of theological maxims. It declared itself solely the captive of the Beloved, God; at the same time it could not get rid altogether of supranaturalistic determinism. Similar to Christian mystics Sufis developed the thesis that Man possessed free will as it was granted to him by the Almighty God, who desired the perfection of His creatures. For Sufis freedom remained a mystery not to be solved by efforts of reason. Djalāl al-Dīn Rūmī wrote:

> There is a disputation (which will continue) till mankind are raised from the dead, between the Necessitarians and the partisans of (Absolute) Free will.
>
> (*Mathnawī*, 6:194)

Since the disputation could not be settled rationally, it should be transferred from the sphere of reason to a sphere where the heart reigns. Man, totally absorbed in his love for God, becomes part of "the ocean"—Absolute Reality and "any action that proceeds from him is not his action, it is the action of the water (of the ocean)" (Rūmī, *Discourses*, p. 55). The overwhelming love for God changes Man so much that the problem of free will becomes insignificant and meaningless. Man is conscious of being united completely with the Absolute Being and then the idea "I am God" naturally arises.

Manṣūr al-Ḥallādj dared utter the bold statement as he came to the conclusion: "If the Spirit is my spirit, and my spirit is His Spirit, then what He wishes I wish, and what I wish He wishes" (*Divān*, p. 75). As regards the prosecution of Ḥallādj and his death sentence, Rūmī wrote, "Some men reckon it as a great pretension; but 'I am God' is in fact a great humility. The man who says 'I am the servant of God' asserts that two exist, one himself and the other God. But he who says 'I am God': that is, 'I am not, He is all, nothing has existence but God, I am pure non-entity, I am nothing." (*Discourses*, pp. 55–56).

Thus, freedom of the will means willing free from external mundane impacts and conforming to the wish of the individual who has known himself and so the Truth. Admitting God's almightiness became but a formal postulate while the practical criterion of morality was personal judgment of what was good. Still, Sufis' free willing was limited and conditioned, as only very few were considered worthy and capable of independent judgment and choice while the majority were obliged to obey their preceptors. Personal volition proved, in fact, to be the volition of spiritual preceptors (saints, sheikhs, etc.).

The right to free judgment was obtained only after passing *ṭarīqa*, the way to perfection. It had to be suffered for, to be obtained through subjecting oneself to austerities, in constant striving to attain the Truth. The adept who had entered the path was expected to ascend through several stations (*maqām*) before he might reach the aim, achieve authentic knowledge of the Truth, be united with the Absolute. The path of perfection is endless:

> I do not know where lead the paths,
> The end of the road is out of view.
> Enough it is for me to know
> That Love will give my footsteps through.
>
> (Ghalib, *Dīwān*, p. 86)

Every believer is on a certain stage of the path leading him to the ideal of perfection. "Not one of us but has a place appointed," proclaims the Koran (Sura 37; 164). Some Muslim mystics enumerate seven states of the soul's purification, which correspond to repentance (*tauba*), turning toward God, ascetism, poverty, patience, *tawakkul* (complete trust in God, and submission to Him), and contentment. At the highest *maqām* the believer comes into a state of ecstasy in which he is conscious of mystical unity with God.

Sufi writings present various descriptions of the stages. Farīd al-Dīn ʿAṭṭār, in his *Manṭiq uṭ-ṭayr* (*The Birds' Conversation*), enumerates seven stages of the mystical path.[9] The first is in the valley of Search (*ṭalab*), where Man is purified from worldly desires and passions and becomes open to the Divine heavenly light; the second is in the valley of love (*ʿishq*), where the mystic life begins (it is the beginning of illumination); the third is in the valley of Apprehension (*ma ʿrifa*), where the mystic is immersed in meditation bringing gnosis; the fourth is in the valley of Detachment/Independence (*istighnā'*), where the soul is enveloped in love for God; the fifth is in the valley of Unification (*tawḥīd*), where the mystic attains to the 'naked,' devoid of any images vision of God and Unity with Him; the sixth is the valley of bewilderment (*ḥayrat*), where all vision disappears and the soul is dazzled with the Divine light; the seventh is in the valley of Annihilation (*fanā'*), where the human self is completely merged in God (F. C. Happold, *Mysticism*, p. 57).

The many-staged way of perfection is an idea found in different religiophilsosphic teachings. Frequently there are seven stages, which may be explained by the sacral character of the number 'seven.' Thus Tibetan Buddhism (*The Book of Golden Precepts*) also stipulates seven stages of the way to perfection. The adept should pass through seven gates, each opened by a golden key. The key of the first gate is kindness, utter charity; that of the second, complete harmony and balance in word and deed; of the third, patience which nothing earthly can disturb; of the fourth, complete indifference to pleasure; of the fifth, spiritual power to attain to supreme Truth; the sixth gate leads to eternal rest and contemplation; while he who can use the seventh key becomes a God and is created a Bodhisattva (ibid., p. 82).

Naturally, the coincidence of numbers is not necessary. The homogeneity of 'ways' in Brahmanism, Buddhism, Taoism, Christian mysticism, or Sufism finds expression in the similarity of their essential characteristics, in an identical perception of goals and means of achieving perfection. The adept entering the path has to get over the duality of the Divine and profane by returning to the Unique Primary Principle.

> The Yogi, is united in identity with the all-pervading, infinite, consciousness, and looks on all with an equal eye, sees the Self present in all beings, and all beings existing in the Self.
>
> ("Bhagavadgītā," p. 150)

Compare also: "If the nature is trained, you may return to *tê* (Virtue) and *tê*[10] at its highest peak is identical with the Beginning" (Chuang-tzu, *Complete Works*, p. 132). And see the turn a poet gives to this idea:

> The whole of me performs that (devotion) which is required by the Path, while keeping the way of that (unity) which was required by my Truth.
>
> And when, no longer separating, I joined the rift, and the fissures caused by the difference of the attributes were closed. . .I knew for sure that we (lover and Beloved) are really One. . .
>
> And my whole was a tongue to speak, an eye to see, an ear to hear, and a hand to seize.
>
> (Ibn al-Fāriḍ, *Ta'iyyat*, pp. 251–52).

Returning to the Oneness (attaining the Truth, the Essential Being) is impossible by rational methods. Al-Ḥallādj said, "La sagesse est par delà le donné actuel, par delà de la borne spatiale, par delà l'intention (de l'intellect), par delà les consciences, par delà les traditions reçues et par delà l'aperception" ("Wisdom is outside of the actual phenomena, outside of space, outside of intentions [of the mind], outside of consciousness, outside of traditions and outside of perception" [L. Massignon, *La passion*, p. 882]).

Methods for 'returning to the Oneness' are various but essentially identical: the correct conduct, abjuration of carnal passions and egoistical wishes, abstemiousness, special physical exercises and breath control, utter self-surrender and concentration. Immersed in himself and detached from all externalities, a mystic learns to discern his physical and spiritual abilities, to regulate them so as to achieve the state of quiet or of peculiar exaltation. He is to liberate himself from his selfish ego and achieve unity with the Absolute: "Reject far away from you the created nature, so that you become He, and He becomes you, really!" taught al-Ḥallādj "Rejette donc loin de toi la nature creé, pour que toi, tu devienne Lui, et Lui, toi, dans la realité" [ibid., p. 845]).

Is perfection of one's personality real or illusory? The science of psychology asserts the need of dialogical communication for Man's development. Mystics practice perpetual dialogue between the individual's self and the Divine Self; this dialoque assists self-consciousness in a certain way since "a person's real life is accessible only to dialogical penetration" (M. M. Bakhtin, *Problemy*, p. 69). Having mastered the methods of Yoga or Sufism one can understand much in oneself as a biological organism and so learn to regulate physiological and psychical processes in it.

Moreover, inner bifurcation of consciousness into the 'present self' and the 'fortuituous self' opens the way to dialogue. But the potentiality of the dialogue depends on the degree in which the 'fortuitous self' is capable of orientation toward perfection. The 'fortuituous self' of the mystical dialogue is a cosmic divine self or the self of the Perfect Man, the Prophet Muḥammad, sometimes the self of a saintly sheikh nearer to mundane circumstances. In the first and second cases too, the dialogue is not productive enough for a collision. A different point of view is necessary for stimulating a person's inner work, reappraising oneself, one's life experiences. In dialogues with God or with Muḥammad, his Prophet, there is no 'collision,' no 'encounter,' no real back-coupling. God and the Prophet are, naturally, passive participants of the dialogue, projections of the personal position of the believer who transfers to the other participant of 'the encounter' what is of importance for himself, the Sufi. Such dialogues may lend some support to self-knowledge, self-conservation, and self-assertion. However, when the 'fortuituous self' is a saint or a sheikh the dialogue seems to be more effective. In this case much depends on the degree of moral perfection of the sheikh or the saint. The history of Sufism evidences frequent occasions of the negative role of 'preceptors,' who acted as 'prophets of decadence' and directed people in the wrong way, leading them away from morality.

It would not be right to evaluate the objective importance of Sufi ethics on the basis of what some Muslim mystics professed. It is only a thorough study of Sufi practice as widely realized within Sufi orders that can result in an equitable appraisal of Sufi moral credo. Orders, unlike earlier Sufi formations, observed a distinct differentiation. As a rule, to be accepted into a Sufi fraternity an adept had to undergo a three-year test of service to sheikh and God. At the initiation an oath was pronounced, its formula something like this: "O God, I have repented before Thee, and accept as my teacher Sheikh X as my sheikh in this world and in the next, as guide and leader to Thy presence, and as a Director in Thy Path. I will disobey him neither in word nor in deed, neither overtly nor covertly. Confirm me, O God, in obedience to him and his *ṭarīqa* in this world and the next" (J. S. Trimingham, *Sufi Orders*, pp. 186–87).

The rules for acceptance into the order Tidjānīyya (nineteenth century) prescribed: "You should absolutely abstain from any other *awrād* (litanies) than those of your sheikh. . . . Do not visit any *walī* (saint) living or dead,[11] for no man can serve two masters. . . . You must not malign, nor bear enmity against your sheikh. . . . You must believe and trust in all that the sheikh says to you about the virtues. . . . You must not criticise any good thing that seems strange to you in this *ṭarīqa*, or you will be deprived of their virtue by the Just Ruler" (ibid., p. 191).

Thus it was that rank-and-file members of Sufi orders, while they got rid of the dictates of official religion as explicated by legal theologians, found themselves dependent upon sheikhs, first of all, and then upon the preceptors of the branch or section appointed by sheikhs (*muqaddam*).

The most negative aspects of Sufism transpired within orders as institutionalized organizations. They were not brought in from outside but integral parts of the double-faced and contradictory worldview of Sufism. Mystics' steering their course toward escape into self was in fact a reaction to the evil, injustice, falsehood, and hypocrisy rampant in society. The tendency of aiming at self-perception and self-perfection furthered in a way an individual's self-assertion and rendered possible a relatively free moral development of personality. On the other hand, escape into self meant practically accepting surrounding reality as impervious to change, admitting the infeasibility of correcting the world of injustice, and hence vindication of social passivity and quietism.

For Sufism perfection consisted in the annihilation of an individual self in the Divine Self. Hence considered objectively, the mystical practice of interiorization could easily result in self-concentration transformed into rummaging within one's soul and chewing one's emotions, while self-perfection turned to yearning for personal salvation.

The idea of the Perfect Man allowed a greater scope for ethical motivation than dogmatic prescriptions. Sufism, with its institution of preceptors and saints, often achieved what the official Islam doctrine failed to do (in Sunni Islam there are no 'living' authorities). In Sufism the Perfect Man—represented by a *walī*, a *nabī*, or a sheikh—fulfills the function of a 'significant friend,' a sort of mirror in which the individual as well as his environment are reflected, a friend who ensures the individual feedback within his immediate social milieu and thus helps orient his behavior in accordance with traditional normative and supernormative systems.

At the same time the ethical credo of Sufism proved not homogeneous but selective. The mass of adepts were obliged to learn the rules and dogmas of Islam, strictly observe *Sharīʿa* prescriptions as the obligatory preliminary condition of entering *Ṭarīqa*, the Path. At the next stage of perfection adepts were still not free in their actions and conduct, having to conform to the guidance of their preceptors in whose presence they "should be as a dead body in the hands of the washer" (F. Rahman, *Islam*, p. 137). Only the elite *'arīfs*, initiates who have attained to the true being and reached the final stage of perfection (*ḥaqīqa*), find moral freedom and may say:

> My degree is of such a height that a man who has not reached it may still be deemed happy; but the state for which I am deemed happy transcends thy degree.
> All men are the sons of Adam, (and I am as they) save that I alone amongst my brethren have attained to the sobriety of union.
> My hearing is like that of Kalim (Moses) and my heart is informed (about God) by the most excellent vision of an eye like that of him who is most excellent.
> And my spirit is a spirit to all the spirits (of created beings); and whatsoever thou seest of beauty in the universe flows from the bounty of my nature.
> Leave, then, to me (and do not ascribe to anyone else) the knowledge with which I alone was endowed before my appearance (in the phenomenal world), while (after my appearance) among created things my friends knew me not (as I really am). . . .
> And let names of honour fall from me and pronounce them not, babbling foolishly, for they are but signs fashioned by one whom I made.
> And take back my title of 'gnostic', for according to the Quarn, if thou approvest people's calling each other names, thou wilt be loathed.
>
> (Ibn al-Fārid *Ta'iyyat*, pp. 229, 231)

4

Sufism and Modernity

The very existence of Sufism implies criticism of and challenge to the orthodox theology.

Fazlur Rahman

Sufism (is) the marrow of the bone or the inner, esoteric dimension of the Islamic revelation.

S. H. Nasr

The great changes introduced to the world by Western civilization have produced different effects on the life of humanity. One of its consequences has been the crisis of religious consciousness. "God is dead!" Friedrich Nietzsche declared to the world exultantly. "Faith in the right ordering of the universe, in humanity, in his own soul and in God, had been destroyed," Leo Tolstoy admitted sadly. "Dieu est mort. . . . Il est mort: il nous parlait et il se tait, nous ne touchons plus que son cadavre" (God is dead. . . . He is dead: He spoke to us and now he is silent, there's only a corpse before us"), Jean Paul Sartre stated.

The crisis of religious consciousness does not necessarily result in taking atheistic positions. Quite often it is not religion that is repudiated but only its traditional form. Then the doctrine gets modernized, its dogmas and postulates adjusted to the novel social situation. But the emphasis on the Deity can also be gradually transferred from the external to the internal, from existence sui generis, now immersed in silence, toward an individual person who can in an encounter with himself discern a hardly audible voice coming from the secret depths of the soul (his own soul). It results in a conspicuous feature of most twentieth-century novel theodicies: the desperate anxiety of their paradoxical, rationally contrived mysticism.

Reanimation of mystical traditions is apparent in the heightened interest in the heritage of early Christian mystics and discussions about it, in attempts to reactualize Gregory of Nyssa's theory of mystic gnosis, in the transition from a transcendental-Thomistic to a personalist-immanent conception of God, in mass yearnings after exotic oriental creeds (and in particular, their mystical elements).

The peculiar sociopolitical and cultural situation in the East 'saved God from death' there. Of primary importance in this has been the general level of development in the countries where the majority of the population still remains deeply devout. In the course of the struggle for independence religious slogans were made use of by national liberation movements because in the East, like in medieval Europe, the sentiments of the masses were fed on religion and it was therefore necessary to put forward their own interests in a religious guise in order to produce an impetuous movement. Besides, oriental creeds symbolized national independence, were reminders of the countries' former (precolonial) greatness, and were opposed to Christianity, the religion of Western conquerors and enslavers. Finally, native religion has fulfilled a consolidating function of sorts; it has been appealed to as an ideology having no concern with class distinctions but unifying different social strata and classes in a single anti-imperialist national force.

The influence of all these factors has been felt up to now. The conservation of religion results from the peculiar character of capitalist development in the former colonial countries, characterized in particular by the existence of polystructural economics and the alienation of huge masses of people from the means of production. These groups of population frequently blame their deteriorating economic conditions on alien Western culture's undermining of the foundations of traditional society. This state of mind tends to sustain established creeds. Hence the tendency for 'religious renascence,' most manifestly prevailing in the countries where the dominant religion is Islam. People are looking for spiritual revival and debates about the Muslim heritage grow increasingly important. In this connection the question of the essence of the Islamic doctrine comes forward as peculiarly critical, and, in particular, determing the place and role of Sufism within Islam.

Traditionally biased Muslims maintain that Sufism is so much in opposition to the spirit and dogma of Islam that it can be considered a heresy or even a quasi-separate religion inadmissible for true believers (F. Rahman, *Islam*, p. 254). The incompatibility of Sufism with Islam is deduced from pantheistic ideas found in mysticism, ideas that "destroyed the Islamic idea of God" (A. Schimmel, *Mystical Dimensions*, p. 263), and also from the Sufi opposition of *maʿrifa* (gnosis, intuitive knowledge) to *ʿilm* (religious knowledge, discursive learning), its undermining of the authority of the *ʿulamāʾ*, its reliance on the teaching of *pīrs*, sheikhs, and *walīs*, and its ethical propensity not to adhere to the formal observance of religious prescriptions (even infractions of them being permissible) but on internal perfection, for adherence to rules and regulations of the *ṭarīqa*. Islamic tradtionalists in general abhorred the nonconformist spirit of Sufism frequently expressed in free thinking, in religious and social protests. That attitude may be provisionally taken as 'right-wing' criticism of Sufism.

The 'left-wing' criticism of Islamic mysticism is perpetrated by modernist thinkers. C. A. Qadir, a prominent Pakistan philosopher, noted that Sufism "not only bred fatalistic tendencies, it also encouraged indifference to social morality. . . .The neglect of social and practical ethics cancelled all programmes of humanitarian activity, left the Muslims far behind in the task of social and political reconstruction" (*Muslim Philosophy*, 2:1432).

M. A. Lahbabi, an Arabian personalist, affirmed: "La retraite de Soufis (sorte de vie monacale particuliere) et le maraboutisme vont a l'encontre de toute evolution culturelle, de tout progres et aussi des directives que donnent le Coran et la Sunna. . . . Presque toutes les pratiques des Soufis sont amusulmanes, quand elles ne sont pas anti-musulmanes" ("Sufis' alienation, a sort of lay monasticism, and indifference to mundane problems are quite contrary to cultural evolution and progress as well as to the prescriptions of the Quran and Sunna. . . . Almost all of Sufis' practices are non-Muslim, unless really anti-Muslim" [*Le personnalisme musulman*, p. 95]).

Thus, both right-wing and left-wing critics of Sufism distinguish it from Islam and believe it is quite out of place to consider even the possibility of using Sufi heritage in the process of solving the problems of modern Muslim society.

Still, there is a different point of view: certain thinkers having nothing to do with either extreme appraise Sufism as part of Islamic tradition and, moreover, think it may prove helpful in dealing with social problems of today. Naturally, there is much variety in cognizance of the problems and, hence, in the appreciation of the Sufi heritage.

It is worthy of note that in the beginning of this century Muslim reformers striving for a radical transformation of oriental society evaluated Sufism quite objectively and clear-headedly. They were aware of the negative aspects of Muslim mysticism. "The emphasis that is laid on the distinction of *ẓāhir* and *bāṭin* (Appearance and Reality) created an attitude of indifference to all that applies to Appearance and not to Reality. This spirit of total otherworldliness in later Sufism obscured men's vision of a very important aspect of Islam as a social polity" (Muhammad Iqbal, *Reconstruction*, p. 150). Reformers hit hardest at Sufi orders' social practice. Muhammad Iqbal charged the orders with having become a bulwark of reaction and spiritual degradation. "The decadents in all ages tried to seek shelter behind self-mysticism and nihilism. . . . Having lost the vitality to grapple with the temporal, these prophets of decay apply themselves to the quest of a supposed eternal, and gradually complete the spiritual impoverishment and physical degeneration of their society by evolving a seemingly charming ideal of life which reduces the healthy and powerful to death" (quoted in S. A. Vahid, *Thoughts and Reflections*, pp. 101–2).

The reformers acknowledged, nevertheless, certain positive apects in Sufism and spoke of its emancipating function. Characteristically, Djamāl al-Dīn Afghānī and Muḥammand ʿAbduh, most prominent representatives of Muslim reformism, began with revering Sufism.[1] When Muḥammad ʿAbduh became dissatisfied with the system of schooling in the famous university of al-Azhar he sought a sheikh and obtained succor from him: "I had found no leader to guide me in that towards which my soul was inclined, except that sheikh who had in a few days delivered me from the prison of ignorance into the open spaces of knowledge, and from the bonds of blind acceptance of authoritative belief (*taqlīd*) into the liberty of the mystic union with God" (in Ch. Adams, *Islam*, p. 25).

In his reconstruction of religious thought in Islam Muḥammad Iqbal borrowed from Sufism what might justify and uphold a dynamic attitude toward life. It was Djalāl al-Dīn Rūmī that Iqbal venerated as his preceptor and chose to be his guide on the path to Reality, to the Truth. It is about Rūmī that Iqbal wrote:

> Bu Ali (Avicenna -M.S.) got lost
> In the dust
> Kicked up by
> Layla's dromedary.
> Rumi's hand
> Seized the curtain
> Of the litter.
> This one dived
> Deeper, deeper still,
> Till he came
> Upon the pearl
> He was after.
> (*Payām-i-mashriq*, p. 67)

Iqbal has been especially attracted by the Sufi idea of the Perfect Man. He has completed, though, the mystic spiritual heroism of *al-insān al-kāmil* by social heroism. While Rūmī's main stages of perfection were belief in God, seeking God, and perception of God through learning the depth of one's own soul, Iqbal adds to that also 'realization,' which becomes possible thanks to 'ceaseless devotion to justice and mercy.' In Iqbal's mind an individual is so independent from God that he may act even as His associate.

The difference of Rūmī's and Iqbal's worldviews is elucidated when we compare these poets' works. Rūmī makes a man sadly conscious of his mistake of relying more upon his equal, 'a created being,' than on God:

> He gave the cap, but Thou the head filled with intelligence.
> He gave the coat, but Thou the tall figure and stature (of its wearer).
> He gave me gold, but Thou the hand that counts gold;
> He gave me the beast for riding, but Thou the mind that rides it.
>
> (*Mathnawī*, 6:431)

In Muḥammad Iqbal's "Conversation of the Creator with Man" the latter says,

> You made the night, and I the lamp,
> And you the clay and I the cup;
> You desert, mountains-peak, and vale;
> I—flower-bed, park, orchard; I
> Who grind a mirror out of stone
> Who brew from poison honey-drink.
> (V. G. Kiernan, *Poems from Iqbal*, p. 94).

When the capacity of God and Man is compared Rūmī shows how insignificant are mortals' doings as compared with God's. Iqbal, on the contrary, underlines the significance of human effort, its productive, creative nature. With Iqbal the individuality, the ego, strives to approach the Divine ego. Yet this striving is not abnegation of one's self but self-assertion: "The ultimate aim of the ego is not to see something, but to be something." The poet-philosopher saw in attaining the proximity of God, or rather the ideal perfection, not an intellectual act but "a vital act which deepens the whole being of the ego, and sharpens his will with the creative assurance that the world is not something to be merely seen or known through concepts, but something to be made and remade by continuous action" (*Reconstruction*, p. 198).

Muhammad Iqbal's Perfect Man is more independent and active than Rūmī's. This discrepancy is entirely natural, caused by the difference of historical periods in which the poets lived and created their works, the disparity of claims time laid upon them.

Iqbal's *al-insān al-kāmil*, to be sure, has greater and further pretensions to a unique role in the universe. Still we must keep in mind that ideas contained in Rūmī's works nourished the philosophical, ethical, and esthetical thought in his own time and in the succeeding centuries up to the present time.[2]

The positive potencies of Sufism were best realized by the Muslim poets. Even poets remote from mystical practices felt the mighty attraction of mysticism as the history of the world literature shows. The best-known among such authors in the European literature are evidently Dante Alighieri, "der zugleich der lezte Dichter des Mittelalters und der erste Dichter der Neuzeit war" ("He who was the last poet of the Middle Ages and the first poet of the new time as well" [Marx, Letter, Bd 22, S. 366]), and Goethe who favored "poetic mysticism." The chance of opposing the official religious doctrine and its institutions, a certain degree of liberation from the authoritative dogmatism and clergy, which impressed artistic consciousness, prevalence given to emotions and intuition contrary to 'cold' rationalism, as well as the sense of Man's inseparable connection with nature, moral self-control in the process of infinite striving for the ideal and ethical perfection[3]—all of these must have agreed with the spiritual disposition of artistic natures.

In the new and modern time concern for mystical philosophy led quite frequently to romanticism with its characteristic concentration on the spiritual and emotional spheres of an individual. This introspection was propelled by the consciousness of an unsolvable tragic contrast between the high ideal and the low reality. Peculiar conditions of romantic art formation in the Muslim countries (unmatched periods and diverse conditions as compared with Europe) determined its direction, which has been rather antifeudal than antibourgeois.[4]

A fine example of mystically colored romanticism is presented by the creative work of Khalil Gibran (1883–1931), a poet, essayist, and artist, whom Mikhail Naʿīmā (1889–1988), another prominent Arab writer, poet, playwright, and critic, called the poet of night, loneliness, ever-watchful spirit, sea and storms, the poet of revolution.

Gibran presents himself to the reader in his essay "The Prophet," the fruit of lifelong search and thinking. The hero of the essay, the prophet al-Mustafa who had waited for twelve years in the city of Orphalese for his ship to return and to bear him back to the isle of his birth, on the eve of leaving the city forever, addresses its people with a parting speech. This predication is a sermon, though in spirit and in form is quite unlike the Koranic one. It is rather like a Sufi's advice, a Sufi's entering the last stage of *fanā'*. "Only another winding will this stream make, only another murmur in this glade, and then shall I come to you, a boundless drop to a boundless ocean" (*Prophet*, p. 10).

The people of the city asked al-Mustafa to speak to them before he left, to give them his truth collected in long wanderings. And the prophet disclosed to them "all that has been shown to him of that which is between birth and death" (ibid., p. 12). The main idea of his ardent prediction is rejecting the humble quiet for the sake of attaining true freedom. "Life is indeed darkness save when there is urge. . . .Verily the lust for comfort murders the passion of the soul" and so let your house "be not an anchor but a mast" (ibid., pp. 31, 39). Only the winged can obtain freedom and attain to the Truth.

> Like the ocean is your god-self;
> It remains forever undefiled.
> And like the ether it lifts but the winged.
> Even like the sun is your god-self;
> It knows not the ways of the mole nor seeks in the holes
> Nor seeks in the holes of the serpent.
>
> (Ibid., p. 45)

The poet proclaims that the soul's passion should be aimed at thwarting the laws that bind it. He compares those who blindly obey the laws and do not understand that life is an ocean and "man-made laws are but sand-towers" to "an ox who loves his yoke," to "an old serpent who cannot shed his skin," to people who "stand in the sunlight, but with their backs to the sun"—"They see only their shadows, and their shadows are their laws" (ibid., pp. 51–52).

But it is not enough to cancel formally the law. The main thing is to feel spiritually free, to banish fear from one's heart. "And if it is a despot you would dethrone, see first that his throne erected within you is destroyed" (ibid., pp. 55–56). Gibran rejects religious dogmas and morals. His prophet edifies the people of Orphalese. "And he who defines his conduct by ethics imprisons his song-bird in a cage"; "Your daily life is your temple and your religion" (ibid., p. 88). Every man's duty is to perceive by himself what is good and what is evil for "the vision of one man lends not the wings to another man" (ibid., p. 65) and each one is lonely in his true knowledge.

Khalil Gibran was not a Sufi[5]; still he employed Sufi ideas, images, and symbols to express protest against stagnation in traditional Muslim society. He longed for revolt, for storms[6] that would let people find their real vocation, obtain real happiness. Gibran's prophet's prediction is constructed of Sufi symbols and, in its spirit, revolutionary, it commends Man the doer, the maker, the creator. It sings the hymn to him: "People of Orphalese, beauty is life when life unveils her holy face. But you are life and you are the veil" (ibid., p. 85). To be worthy of Man's name impersonating Beauty and Life one must work, as Life is work, labor done with love and inspiration. To work with love is

> to weave the cloth with threads drawn from your heart,
> even as if your beloved were to wear that cloth;
> It is to build a house with affection,
> even as if your beloved were to dwell in that house.
> It is to sow seeds with tenderness and reap the harvest with
> joy, even as if your beloved were to eat the fruit.
>
> (Ibid., p. 32)

Gibran's preaching of "loving life through labour" and thus approaching God, the deepest mystery of Being, coincides with the Protestant principle of labor being honorable and pleasing to God, to that novel idea of God maintained by Luther (the Creator prizes most in Man a diligent, steady, and enterprising worker), which created in medieval Europe initial premises for a religiomoral elevation of success in private enterprise that corresponded to the requirements of developing bourgeois economic structure.

Many prone to reforms find Sufism a most convenient form for expressing the intention to refashion the social structure and the rejection or transformation of obsolete religious traditions inhibiting the social change. While these people do not see Sufism as a universal expedient, still they believe that elements of love of freedom contained in Islamic mysticism, its spirit of moral perfection, may be of use in motivating social action and progress.

It is possible, of course, to see the way to perfection quite differently, that is, not by means of radical innovations, reforms, or break-throughs to the future, but by the revival of the lost ideal. In that case Sufism looks like the concentrated essence of Islam, the kernel of Islam, its metaphysical doctrine.

In the works of S. H. Nasr, the best known Muslim philosopher outside the world of Islam, or F. Schuon and M. Ling, both sharing similar views, there is a persistent insistence on Sufism being the true essence of Muslim creed since it is the central and most mighty part of the wave that is revelation. "The strictly Quranic and Muhammedan character of the Sufic way" enables one to "say that Sufism is orthodox thrice over" as compared with traditional theological doctrine (F. Schuon, *Understanding Islam*, pp. 154, 138).

Islamic mysticism is presented as a changeless and timeless creed. Nasr wrote, "One cannot properly speak of a history of Sufism because in its essence Sufism has no history." And again, "One cannot speak in an ordinary historical sense about the origin and sources of the work of any Sufi writer because the Sufi who has realized the goal of the Path receives inspiration directly and 'vertically' and is not dependent upon 'horizontal influences' " (*Three Muslim Sages*, pp. 84–85, 100).

According to Nasr, Sufism "is timeless. . . based on elements of reality both transcendent and immanent within human nature which neither evolve nor decay" (ibid., p. 35). And again, "Because it (Sufism) is concerned with the perennial and the universal, Sufism remains as relevant today as in every past age" (ibid., p. 39).

There is no doubt that such categorical negation of historical determination and of the evolution of Sufi ideas can be disputed. However, it is more important to understand why Nasr and those who think like he are so persistent in their accentuation of the perennial character of Sufism.

The easiest explanation is that their objection to any changes in the world of Islam is motivated by the desire to keep it free from any influences from the outside and from the West, in particular. In that case their position looks openly conservative. But this explanation does not agree with that search for justification of the vital necessity of the development of sciences and new technologies for the Muslims so typical of Nasr.

By reading the works of the Iranian philosopher more attentively one is prone to think that Nasr's appeal to Sufism has been motivated by the desire to discover for Muslim countries such a way of modernization, of the acceptance and utilization of the achievements of modern science and technology, that could lead to preservation of their cultural identity, the values and the ideals of Islamic civilization. But then it could be asked: Is this desire to limit the influence of sciences by material production realistic, or is there any chance for sciences to develop in the framework of the medieval world outlook? It is this very problem that practically all the traditional societies so painfully try to solve.

There could be another explanation for this stress on the perennial character of Sufism. Presentation of the latter as being determined neither by time nor space helps reduce Islam's confrontation with other religious beliefs, to exclude from the teaching of Muḥammad a political ferment nourishing the aggressive fanaticism of Islamic fundamentalism. This statement could be confirmed by at least two examples.

The first one is the lecture delivered by T. O. Ling in 1981, "Religion without Radical Theology," issued as a booklet with the title *Islam's Alternative to Fundamentalism*. Ling, professor of comparative religion in the University of Manchester, made apparent the intention of certain circles within the Islamic world and still more of those beyond it, to make use of Sufism as an alternative to fundamentalism or, otherwise designated, Islamic revivalism. Why was Sufism selected? Primarily because in Muslim countries any non-Islamic creed would be rejected because of intense nationalist and, correspondingly, anti-Western predispositions. Sufism is, on the contrary, a growth of Islamic spiritual culture itself, prized for its supposed estrangement from politics, alienation from the world, and mundane troubles and problems. It is counterpoised to the traditional doctrine so closely concerned with political issues (up to sustaining the indivisibility of religion and state). Ling elucidated, "It is precisely at such a time of political polarization that a non-political contemplative theology could play an important neutral role" (*Islam's Alternative*, p. 175).

The other example is the international seminar on Sufism that took place in New Delhi in December 1991. The very fact that the seminar was organized as part of the centennary celebrations of Abul Kalam Azad, well-known for his efforts to reduce the communal tension between Hindus and Muslims, as well as the orientation of the majority of the papers presented by the participants from India, proves that there were not only academic but also political motives behind its arrangement: to appeal to Sufism as a means of reconciling Hindus and Muslims in India.

There is no doubt a great deal of affinity between Sufism and the mystical teachings of other religious beliefs. This likeness can be helpful in preventing religiopolitical confrontations. Besides, a mystical teaching directs people toward individual perfection, keeping away from mundane affairs, and that also promotes peacemaking processes.

However, it will be unjustified to create illusions. It is not reasonable to ignore the history that shows that Sufism as a religiophilosophical trend (not as a phenomenon of ascetism or of mystical experience) quite often played political roles. It is generally acknowledged that Sufism many times served as a form of expressing social discontent, disobedience to the dominant lay and spiritual authority. Even in its passive indifference to politics, it accomplished certain political functions by distracting attention from lay problems, thus helping those in power maintain the establishment.

To appraise Sufism objectively it is necessary to study its history, taking into consideration all the aspects of the matter, to examine it in its dialectical development. Absolutization of certain aspects of this trend to the exclusion of others distorts the picture.

Idealization of Islamic mysticism, regarding it as a kind of savior for humanity, does not seem productive either. One can understand the true believer's estimation of Sufism as "a grace from Heaven and a sign of Divine Mercy (*raḥmān*) not only for Muslims but also for non-Muslims" as "the net that prevents a fall into the bottomless pit of the inferior waters" (Nasr, *Sufi Essays*, p. 41). The belief is always above boundaries and conditions. But does not this statement contain a danger of peremptory arrogance and hence of a confrontation with the others being no less sincere in their beliefs? And if we want to live in peace and prosperity should we not (for our sake as well as for the sake of all the others) take profit from those potentials of Sufism that promote peace and provide cultural dialogue? As the Great Sheikh said:

> the believer praises the Divinity which conforms to his own belief and connects himself to it in this way; but, all acts return to their author, so that the believer praises himself, as the work praises its artist, all perfection and all lack that it manifests falling back on its author. In the same way, the Divinity (as such, which) conforms to the belief is created by he who concentrates on It, and It is his own work. In praising that which he believes, the believer praises his own soul, it is because of that he condemns other beliefs than his own; if he was just, he would not do it. . . . It he understood the sense of the word of Djunayd: 'The colour of water is the colour of its receptacle', he would admit the validity of all beliefs, and he would recognise God in every form and every object of faith. (*Wisdom of the Prophets*, p. 132)

Appendix

After *Philosophical Aspects of Sufism* was published in 1987, this theme was further investigated in Russia in two Ph.D. theses. The first of these was dedicated to "classical" Muslim mystical thought, while the aim of the second study was to find out whether Sufism had relevance for today's Muslim socieities.

Odd as it may seem, the name of Ibn ʿArabī was touched upon in Soviet Sufi studies only in passing, if mentioned at all. And although al-Sheikh al-Akbar did become the "main hero" of *Philosophical Aspects of Sufism*, it was never the task of that book to concentrate exclusively on this monumental figure and to press an exhaustive analysis of his philosophical ideas. Such a task could only be carried out by a scholar who had mastered Arabic.

Andrey Smirnov. Philosophy of Ibn ʿArabī. Ph.D. Thesis (Philosophy). Institute of Philosophy, USSR Academy of Sciences. Moscow, 1989.

The Ph.D. thesis presented by Andrey V. Smirnov is based on the scrupulous investigation of the two major works of the Great Sheikh, *Fuṣūṣ al-ḥikam* (*Gems of Wisdom*) and *al-Futūḥāt al-Makkiya* (*Meccan Revelations*). The first of these was translated into Russian and commented on by Smirnov.

In his Ph.D. thesis Smirnov makes an attempt to present Ibn ʿArabī's ideas in the form of an integral philosophical system. Scholars acquainted with the texts of the Great Sheikh would agree that such a task is far from easy. Neither *Fuṣūṣ al-ḥikam* nor *al-Futūḥāt al-Makkiya* offers a logical structure and a systematic presentation as far as philosophical ideas are concerned. Moreover, too many issues are discussed in different contexts and varying (sometimes even contradictory) solutions are offered. There needs to be an integrated study of Ibn ʿArabī's philosophy, Smirnov stresses, if one wants to understand adequately each of Sheikh's theses, while such an idea results from comprehensive understanding of all his views. The first step in comprehending the Great Sheikh's philosophy would be unbending this hermeneutic circle.

Hence, the primary task is to get an idea of an overall schema underlying Ibn ʿArabī's philosophical exploration. This task being accomplished, one could read his texts anew, testing and correcting the primary logical schema, while the adjusted schema would, in turn, make it possible to reach a higher level of understanding.

To adopt such a procedure Smirnov assumes that, first, there is such an overall logical scheme of Ibn ʿArabī's philosophy, and second, that one can attain it not only from his texts. Both assumptions are, of course, only hypotheses. The second one is true only if the phenomenon called "medieval Arab philosophy" is homogeneous, this homogeneity being based on fact that the logic of building a philosophical system common to all medieval Arab philosophers prevails over heterogeneous influences.

The analysis of the major schools of medieval Arab philosophy (Kalām, Aristotelianism, and Ismā ʿīlīyya) verifies the homogeneity hypothesis. The common logical basis for the philosophical discourse of these schools is formulated as a set of fundamental problems that any philosopher of that time had to pose in order to proceed with a philosophic explanation of the universe.

The differences among the above-mentioned schools boiled down to initially different solutions to these basic problems. Moreover, the development of medieval Arab philosophical thought has proved to be logically consistent: each new attempt undertaken to solve these basic problems (and thus constituting a new major trend) is aimed at overcoming the contradictions of the previous one. Within the framework of such an understanding of the process of historical development of philosophy the concept of paradigm is relevant, thought in this case it is applied in a sense rather different from that introduced by T. S. Kuhn.

If we understand philosophy as a dialogue of thinkers stretching through the centuries, Smirnov argues, then a study in the field of the history of philosophy is an attempt to comprehend the contents of this dialogue. To begin with, we must understand the premises underlying the philosophers' mutual questions and answers, the premises that are mostly implicit, not explicit, in their philosophical discourse. What is meant by a paradigm in this study is the hidden basis making a philosophical question possible. To ask what it is or why it is so one should first be convinced that it *is*. Such a conviction shared by all the philosophers of the period in question is a starting point in determining the type of questions asked and setting quite certain (though rather wide, of course) limits to the answers that may be given. Furthermore, it is this starting point, this paradigm of questioning and answering, which establishes the ultimate criteria for the coherence of the philosophical system, for what is usually referred to as its "logical consistency."

Thus Smirnov concludes that a study of the historical development of philosophical thought can be undertaken with the help of the paradigmatic method.

He believes that the paradigmatic study of medieval Arab philosophy provides a necessary key for deciphering the philosophical texts of Ibn ʿArabī. Many scholars have noted that the sheikh's philosophy is far from homogeneous. Perhaps a metaphor of a multimeasure space is appropriate to describing this peculiarity of the Great Sheikh's thought: reading his texts one gets the impression of invisible bounds that stand in the way of linking different problems together, as if these bounds cannot be surpassed by mere logical reasoning; sometimes two or three different solutions to the problem are given in the same context without any explicit explanation of such diversity. This fact is usually either ignored altogether or declared to be a result of the author's inner contradictions or the impossibility of incorporating mystical experience within the narrow frames of philosophical discourse.

All such explanations have one trait in common: they proceed from the presumption that it would be "unnatural" for one philosophical system to consist of parallel (in some sense even incompatible) levels of thought and thus to strive to eliminate this fact one way or another. But quite the opposite must be done. Smirnov believes that to understand Ibn ʿArabī's philosophy this diversity of levels of thought must be made the fundamental principle of explanation.

This approach proceeds from the assumption that there are three kinds of cognition which, to put it in modern terms, exhaust all the possible relations between subject and object (first, independence; second, partial merger; third, indistinguishability. Different levels of Ibn ʿArabī's thought are represented by philosophical knowledge resulting from these three kinds of cognition; a notion of *philosophema* is adopted to denote each of these levels.

Thus the overall system of Ibn ʿArabī is described as consisting of three philosophemas, each of them giving a systematic explanation of the universe adequate to what is required by the paradigm of medieval Arab philosophy.

The three philosophemas and the three kinds of cognition (rational, intuitive, and mystical) corresponding to them are not just mechanically joined together to make up an overall philosophical system. Their synthesis is organic, and as such it demands a special element not incorporated by synthesized subsystems (i.e., philosophemas) but linking them in an integral system. Such a synthesizing element in the Great Sheikh's philosophy seems to be the conception of the "new creation" (*al-khalq al-djadīd*). Within the framework of an integral system the philosophemas gain a content somewhat richer than that disclosed by analytical investigation.

Smirnov analyzes the structure and content of Ibn ʿArabī's integral philosophical system. Among others the problems of the atomic structure of time, the relation between the temporal and the eternal, and the implications of these conceptions for Ibn ʿArabī's theory of causality are investigated.

A number of peculiar philosophical categories used by Ibn ʿArabī are discussed and a rather uncommon understanding of them is proposed. These categories are the sense (*ma'nan*), Self-ness (*dhāt*), relation (*nisba*), corelation (*iḍāfa*), and several others.

First, Smirnov argues that an adequate understanding of these categories has nothing to do with an attempt (so often undertaken) to treat them as related to the opposition of ideal-material, or real-unreal. What Ibn ʿArabī says is that there is no opposition between eternal and temporal, God and world, but each of the two is equally necessary for the other to exist. Ibn ʿArabī stresses that one cannot avoid inconsistency in contemplating God philosophically without the concept of temporal worldly existence being from the very beginning present in this contemplation. For such an explanation to be possible there need to be categories describing the initial unity of eternal and temporal.

Trying to find such categories in Ibn ʿArabī's vocabulary, Smirnov looks at the word *ma'nan*. The best rendering of this term, in his opinion, would be "sense," not "meaning." The meaning is something that is hidden behind a denoting sign, always related (and thus secondary) to it and belonging to a domain basically different from that of the sign. Sense brings to mind an idea of something "self-sufficient." The sense may be not meant or denoted, but it exists "by itself."

The category sense in Ibn ʿArabī's philosophy is closely linked (but not opposed) to form (*ṣūra*). The sense may equally have form and be devoid of it. Form is a limited sense, the sense on which the bounds of temporal and spatial existence have been imposed. In the God's Self all the senses are unlimited, have no form, and thus are merged together, unseparated from one another; acquiring the form they become "embodied" (*muta ʿayyina*) as the worldly essences (*ʿayn*).

The Divine Self (*Dhāt*) proves to be an absolute abundance of the senses because of an infinite number of inner relations (*nisab*), which serve for Ibn ʿArabī as a principle of differentiation of God's unity. The term *nisba* is mostly (though not always) used in his texts to denote an inner relation in God (that is to say, a relation that is contemplated before the related essences) while *iḍāfa* refers to a corelation between the "unformed" sense in God and the "formed" one in the world. Any essence (the "formed," or definite sense) of the world is corelated with a sense in God, thus making it possible, as Ibn ʿArabī stresses, to use any noun, adjective, or pronoun for denoting the inner senses of God.

The process of "forming" (*taṣwīr*) the sense, if we consider only a single sense (or a limited number of them), is called *ta'ayyun* (embodiment), and when regarded in its full scope (that is, as an embodiment of all the senses in God), it is called Self-manifestation (*al-tadjallī al-dhātī*). The reverse process, the process of transgressing the formal limitations that the senses bear in their temporal existence, is called *al-taḥaqquq*. This category, Smirnov believes, is best translated as "realization," that is, acquiring unity with the Real (*al*-Ḥaqq, the God). Since Man is an all-encompassing creature (*al-kawn al-jāmi'*) embodying all the senses that are to be found in God, the realization is always possible. A mystic who has reached this stage of unity is called *al-mutaḥaqqiq bi-l-ḥaqq*, "the one who has realized the Reality of the Real and by the Real."

It is the sense that expresses the initial unity of what in terms of Western philosophy may be denominated as ontological and epistemological. To realize the sense means both to be and to know. The God, the continuity of Self-existence, is always unveiled as a multiplicity of definite senses. The sense itself is manifested in the world, not the "material" as a denotation of sense. Understanding something (*fahm*) means realizing in one's self the same reality that is embodied in that thing as a limited (i.e., definite) sense, and "what is understood" (*mafhūm*) is the thing itself, not an (ideal) "meaning" of that thing. Following the mainstream of Ibn ʿArabī's thought we discover a rather unusual way of discussing traditional philosophical questions, Smirnov says.

From the point of view adopted in this study, Ibn ʿArabī's philosophy is evaluated as a climax of medieval Arab thought. It demonstrated that the prime ontological problem of transcendence and immanence of the principle of existence (God) to the realm of existent things (the world) has no solution in traditional terms. If God is contemplated, in accordance with the paradigm of medieval thought, as the only self-existent essence bearing in this respect no semblance to imperfect temporal world then existence of the existent is in no way possible. This is what Ibn ʿArabī says: the principle of existence may not be other than the existent itself.

This conclusion in fact denies the medieval paradigm and outlines totally new perspectives for philosophy. After Ibn ʿArabī, a new mode of thinking was needed.

The actual history of philosophical thought is far, Smirnov believes, from exhausting all of the virtual possibilities to construct philosophical knowledge that are opened at each of its stages. The paradigmatic method proves to be effective in disclosing such lines of development which, though not realized actually, were nevertheless prepared by the preceding history of thought. In this thesis such virtual possibilities for further development of Arab philosophy, based on Ibn ʿArabī's ideas, are analyzed.

Kamila Hromova. The Critical Analysis of Seyyed Hossein Nasr, a Modern Iranian Philosopher. Ph.D. Thesis (Philosophy). Institute of Philosophy, USSR Academy of Sciences. Moscow, 1988.

The name of Seyyed Hossein Nasr has been mentioned in quite a number of books and articles published in Russian over the past two decades. Some aspects of his outlook were examined by S. M. Aliev, V. N. Vorobieva, E. A. Doroshenko, N. C. Kirabaev, V. B. Klyashtorina, I. O. Kozlova, L. R. Polonskaya, and A. V. Sagadeev. However, Kamila Hromova's Ph.D. thesis is the first attempt of a *philosophical* analysis of Nasr's views. It is important to note here that in contrast to the majority of the above-mentioned authors Hromova's study treats Nasr as a philosopher rather than as a religious ideologist. Hence she succeeds in avoiding oversimplifications like assigning the Iranian thinker to the ranks of Muslim 'traditionalists,' 'orthodoxes,' or 'bourgeois theorists of Islam.'

Hromova examines Nasr's philosophy in the wide context of confrontation between Islamic culture and modern sciences and technology. In her opinion the views of Nasr, who had been closely connected with the Shah's regime, developed under the direct influence of the sociopolitical situation, where the monarchy, being in its form traditional, in essence played the role of the promoter of modernization in Iranian society.

Hromova points out that, on the one hand, the Shah and his associates made efforts to maintain the influence of Muslim tradition and the symbols of the belief, trying to sanctify the reforms carried out by them. On the other hand, aiming at the capitalist transformation of society, they fully realized the necessity of corresponding changes in Islamic ideology. Besides, they faced the oppostion on behalf of the shia' clergy as the latter were losing economic and political positions in the process of the reforms. The clergy managed to unite under their banner many of those whose material and social status had been destroyed by the rapid development of capitalism in Iran. Hence it was necessary to limit the influence of Islam so that the clergy would remain only as a religious authority without being involved in politics.

The Shah and the people of his circle were interested in developing sciences, both experimental and theoretical, because they were aware that without the latter there was no guarantee of success in economic development. At the same time they were inclined to reduce the influence of sciences to the sphere of material production, excluding their impact from the area of ideology.

Hromova regards Nasr's philosophy as an effort to solve the problems associated with the inclusion of Muslim society, in particular, Iranian, in modern civilization. He rejects blind imitation of foreign experience and world outlook; he strives to discover the stimulus for progress *inside* Islamic culture itself, trying to find out and advance to the forefront those of its elements that are able to be sufficiently flexible, open to adjustment to other cultures.

Keeping this purpose in mind, Nasr turns to the mystical trend of thought in Islam, as he considers Sufism to represent the *living* tradition of Islam.

Hromova believes that Nasr has replaced Islamic tradition by a Sufi interpretation of the ontological and ethical aspects of the interrelation of God and Man. His concept of Man proceeds from the distinction between the Absolute and the relative (*Sufi Essays*, p. 129). Hromova points out that Nasr rejects the pantheistic character of the Sufi concept of the Unity of Being. He states that "the Absolute is at once Being and above-Being" (ibid., p. 18). He rejects pantheism, as it logically leads to negation of transcendental being.

At the same time, according to Hromova, Nasr appeals, in fact, to pantheistic ideas in formulating his own anthropological conception (*Poiski*, p. 161). Examining Nasr's vision of Man's place and role in the universe, Hromova notes that the pontifical nature of Man "transcends him and. . .yet is none other than his own inner nature" (*Knowledge*, p. 161). Having his 'roots' in transcendental reality, Man always feels a need to be reborn "in the spiritual world with its infinite horizons and delivered from the prison of contingency and the finiteness of the terrestial world that surround him" (*Sufi Essays*, p. 36). As Nasr points out, "to be human means to want to transcend the merely human" (ibid., p. 27). Hence there is Man's mystical quest for the Absolute and the Perennial.

In short, Man is "the vicegerent of God on earth"; he plays "his role as an intermediary between Heaven and earth" (*Knowledge* pp. 160–61). Pontifical Man is born to know the Absolute and to live according to the will of Heaven (ibid., p. 180).

Nasr opposes the modern conception of Man, which "envisages him as the Promethean earthy creature who has rebelled against Heaven" (*Knowledge*, p. 160). Promethean Man is weak and forgetful; he surrenders to the influence of the material, secular world. He cuts himself away from celestial and immutable archetype and becomes "purely terrestrial" (*Sufi Essays*, p. 85). As a result Man loses the true orientation in the world; he falsely accepts the environment, the changing aspects of things, as the only existing reality. In this metaphysical mistake one should see the roots of the main worldview in the West, which is based solely on the changing aspects of things (ibid., p. 86).

Nasr thinks that the tragedy of modern Man consists in his naive belief that he can bring perfection by the total reformation of the earthy, finite existence, which results in damage to nature, in ecological crises. Nasr believes that it is Sufism that "serves essentially the function of reminding man of who he really is," reminds him" to seek all that he needs inwardly within himself, to tear his roots from the outer world and plunge them in the Divine Nature, which resides at the center of his heart" (ibid., p. 33).

By analyzing Nasr's works Hromova comes to the conclusion that his understanding of perfection means getting the knowledge of the truth discovered in revelation and bringing human life into conformity with religious prescriptions (*Ideals*, p. 28). She perceives some similarities between Nasr's views and those of humanitarian anthropologists in contemporary philosophy. Both attribute the failure of the development of essential human potentialities and the creation of social crises to the nature of human consciousness (*Poiski* p. 168).

Hromova warns against prematurely reckoning Nasr among the unconditional opponents of social modernization. She defines his understanding of modernization not as the adoption of Western values and institutions but as the search for the ways and methods of organizing life in conformity with the Truth (*Ideals*, p. 98), that is, in harmony with the standards and the ideals of Islamic civilization. The latter is seen as a certain structural unity of that which is permanent, 'immutable,' with that which is changing, historically concrete (*Poiski*, p. 172).

Hromova believes that though Nasr insists on the organization of life in accordance with Islamic traditions, he never means by that the revival of the norms and institutions of the medieval past (in contrast to the Muslim fundamentalists). He maintains that socio-historical, transient situations are not determined by men, but by the will of destiny (*Ideals*, p. 98). That is why Muslims are in need of individual spiritual perfection rather than of activity aimed at social transformation.

According to Nasr, the highest means of spiritual attainment is sacred knowledge (*Knowledge*, p. 316). How can one gain access to that knowledge? The obvious response would be through tradition. However, this answer is not sufficient for Nasr. As he writes: "Since sacred knowledge deals with matters of a veritable esoteric nature which, even in a traditional context, cannot be taught to everyone. . . such a knowledge can never be divorced from ethics" (ibid., p. 316). Only the 'master' knows and can teach others, the master who has climbed the dangerous path of the cosmic mountain to its peak and who can instruct others to do the same (ibid., p. 317).

Hromova comes to the conclusion that by accentuating Sufism as the sacred tradition of Islam Nasr in a certain way transforms religious ideology: he focuses attention not so much on following rituals and formal prescriptions as on ethics. The priority is clearly given to Man's orientation towards 'universal' ideals and values over strict adherence to the norms of *Sharī'a*. Such reorientation, Hromova believes, gives chances to the critical interpretations of some Islamic prescriptions, mainly those belonging to the areas of politics and economics, which place obstacles to the transformations, to the adjustments in accordance with the challenge of modern times (*Poiski*, p. 176).

Examining Nasr's views on belief and knowledge, religion and science, Hromova points out that he often criticizes modern Man for 'ignorance,' for a secular vision of nature in which there is no place left for God (*Encounter*, p. 20). Nasr maintains that ecological crises and the other negative consequences of rationalism could be overcome by the synthesis of science and religion.

Nasr does not accept the division of the spheres of influence between science and religion, which justifies secularization of nature. Proceeding from the Sufi concept of Man, according to which he is a microcosm reproducing the structure of the universe-macrocosm, Nasr ranks reason as a hierarchical 'level' of human reality proceeding from the intellect. The latter is associated with intuition, not rationality. Hence Nasr prefers to call it "intellectual intuition which involves the illumination of the heart and the mind of man and the presence in him of knowledge of an immediate and direct nature which is tasted and experienced" (*Knowledge*, p. 130).

Intellectual intuition is a quality of Man's divine nature. However, "man is from this primordial nature to be able to make full use of this divine gift by himself. He needs revelation which alone can actualize the intellect in man" (ibid., p. 148). Intellect is a means of getting the knowledge of the highest Reality, the Absolute. As to reason and sciences, they give the knowledge of the phenomenal world.

According to Nasr, reason's vision of reality is of two types. One is 'naturalistic' or 'factual'; the other is 'symbolic.' The first lays the foundation for natural sciences; the second, for cosmological ones. As the 'naturalistic' and 'cosmological' sciences deal with the ontologically different aspects of reality, they represent separate, qualitatively distinct kinds of knowledge.

The natural sciences study the 'material' aspect of the reality in its multiplicity and permanent alterations. That is why these sciences embody a developing knowledge, which discovers and stores data concerning nature. Meanwhile the cosmological sciences reflect the eternal and the immutable side of things. The existence of these two kinds of knowledge is at the same time justified and vital; hence they should exist in parallel. Nevertheless, this parallelism does not exclude the hierarchy in which naturalistic knowledge gets the lowest rank.

Nasr sees the way to the harmonious synthesis of Islam with science in the creation of a hierarchical system of different types of knowledge. He suggests the system consists of three main levels.

Metaphysics is at the top, as its knowledge is acquired by intellectual intuition. Metaphysics is the highest science of reality, the only one capable of seeing the difference between the Absolute and the Relative, the Real and the Phenomenal (*Encounter*, p. 81). In fact, metaphysics expounds the general principles of the Islamic 'world outlook'; it presents a certain system of value ordinates in accordance with which Muslims should look at the world and at all that is happening in it (*Poiski*, p. 194).

The natural sciences belong to the lowest level, as they deal with the material world. The object of the natural sciences is this world, as the reflection of God. That is why these sciences are nothing but the reflection of metphysics, the knowledge of the Divine.

The cosmological sciences are in between. Hromova points out that many Soviet scholars are of the opinion that Nasr rejects modern sciences and strives to replace them with traditional Islamic sciences. Hromova considers that erroneous. She writes: "If we study Nasr's works more profoundly, it will come out that his intention is to present the Medieval Islamic sciences not as alternatives to the modern sciences but as an intermediate level between them and the 'Oriental Wisdom' or metaphysics in order to 'neutralize' those Weltanschauung conclusions which could be made on the basis of discoveries of the modern sciences" (*Poiski*, p. 195).

Cosmological and 'factual' sciences draw information from the same sensual data. However, the former looks at them in the light of supersensual experience. Cosmological sciences apply to the sensual data the metaphysical scale of coordinates. As a result, the natural phenomena, which Man can observe in everyday life, start to play the role of religious symbols.

Nasr applies to natural sciences *ta'wil*, that is, a method used in Sufism for hermeneutic interpretation of the Koran. He believes that this method is very effective when Islam is challenged by the theories of Copernicus or Darwin. Both the geocentric and the evolutionary theories seem to be incompatible with the religious picture of the world until 'a new vision' of the physical world goes together with a new 'spiritual vision' (*Encounter*, p. 66).

Hromova states that according to Nasr 'symbolical' interpretation is applied to the knowledge that is 'given,' received through experiments, rationalization, and systematization. Thus the process of getting a new knowledge and its testing 'falls out' from 'secular' sciences by understanding that the reality that they study is only a 'lower,' material part of the reality as such. That is why his conclusions, if they come into contradiction with religious views, should not get the status of ideological orientations.

Hromova believes that rejecting secularization of sciences formally, nevertheless Nasr advocates it unconsciously. In fact, he comes back to the point from which he started. He wished to avoid the split between modern science and religion. But by acknowledging the right of science for a criterion for the truth, separate from religion, Nasr thus recognizes the autonomy of science.

In Hromova's opinion, Nasr suggests utilitarian attitude toward modern science by explaining to a Muslim how he should live, if he wants to remain pious and at the same time profit from the modern achievements of sciences and technology (*Poiski*, p. 199).

Perhaps Hromova's conclusions and appraisals are not always justified and well grounded. It is noteworthy that they are better argued in the above book than in her Ph.D. thesis. There is no doubt that more profound study of the works by an outstanding Muslim philosopher of the modernity will bring us closer to an adequate explication of his views as well as to their more constructive critical comprehension.

Notes

Introduction

1. A survey of Sufi studies in Russia is given by A. Knysh, a historian from St. Petersbourg, in *Islam: An Outline of the History of Islamic Studies*, edited by S. M. Prozorov, Moscow, "Nauka," 1991 (pp. 125–28, 149–54). The survey contains valuable information about the main trends in Russian Sufi studies. However, the author's estimations are stamped sometimes by subjectivity.

2. S. L. Frank (1877–1950) is one of the most prominent Russian philosophers of this century. He was closely connected with such outstanding religious thinkers as Sergey Bulgakov and Nikolay Berdyaev. In 1922 Frank was expelled from the Soviet Union along with the other famous Russian intellectuals. He spent his exile life in Germany, France, and England. Among Frank's significant works are *Downfall of Idols* (1924); *Meaning of Life* (1926); and *The Unknowable: An Ontological Introduction to the Philosophy of Religion* (1938). The latter was translated into English by B. Jakim and published by London-Ohio, University Press, in 1983.

3. It may be useful to recall here how Engels, brought up in the atmosphere of religious orthodoxy and piety, became an atheist. His way to the rejection of religious dogmatism and later of religious belief as such was hard and painful. In a letter to a former schoolmate, Friedrih Graeber, dated 12–27 July 1839, ninteen-year-old Engels wrote: "I pray daily, indeed nearly the whole day, for truth, I have done so ever since I began to have doubts, but I still cannot return to your faith. And yet it is written, 'Ask, and it shall be given you.' I search for truth wherever

I have hope of finding even a shadow of it and still I cannot acknowledge your truth as the eternal truth. And yet it is written: 'Seek, and ye shall find.'. . .Tears come into my eyes as I write this. I am moved to the core, but I feel I shall not be lost; I shall come to God, for whom my whole heart yearns." (*Collected Works*. Vol. 2, p. 461.)

4. Lenin believed the formula "Religion is the opium of the people" was "the corner stone of the whole Marxist outlook on religion" (V. Lenin, *The Attitude of the Workers' Party to Religion*, pp. 402–03).

5. Among the works published in Russia in the past decade are R. Fish, *Djalāl al-Dīn Rūmī*, Moscow, 1985; V. Braginski, *Hamza Fansuri*, Moscow, 1988; *Sufism in the Context of the Muslim Culture*, ed. N. Prigarina, Moscow, 1985; articles dedicated to Sufism in the *Encyclopedic Dictionary*, Moscow, 1991.

6. I am of course aware of the great difference of opinion concerning Ibn ʿArabī, including those who state that starting with al-Sheikh Al-Akbār the degeneration of *tasawwuf* had begun.

7. I agree with Ye. E. Bertels in his confutation of "indivisible Sufism" but cannot condone his negative attitude toward attempts to construct a general scheme of Sufi doctrine (see *Sufism and Sufi Literature*, p. 226). Such attempts are not only permissible and justified, but most necessary for elucidating general descriptions that let Sufism be attributed to a definite trend in the spiritual culture of Muslim peoples. It seems appropriate to recollect here Hegel's words: "This kind of thing inevitably happens with any historical work which tries to cover long periods or indeed the whole of world history; it is compelled to dispense more or less with individual accounts of reality and to make do with abstractions, summaries and abridgments. This means not only that many events and actions must be omitted, but also that thought or understanding, the most effective means of abridgment, must intervene" (*Philosophy of the World History*, p. 18).

Chapter One. Unity of Being

1. L. Massignon in his article on *tasawwuf* states that adepts of the concept of 'Unity of Being,' called "*wudjūdiyya*," represented the dominant school in the final stage of Sufi doctrinal development (see *Shorter Encyclopaedia of Islam*, p. 581).

2. The idea was shared, more or less, by Sufis preceding Ibn ʿArabī, as evidenced in the utterances of Bisṭāmī Abū Yazīd (d. 874)

and Manṣūr al-Ḥallādj (d. 922), and the poetry of the Egyptain anchorite Ibn al-Fāriḍ (1180–1234). The term *wạhdat al-wudjūd* was first used in systematic fashion by Sa'īd al-Dīn al-Kūnawī (d. 1300), a disciple of Ṣadr al-Dīn al-Kūnawī, himself a disciple of Ibn ʿArabī (see W. C. Chittick, *Sufi Path of Knowledge*, p. 243).

3. It is in the first, 'cosmic' sense that the Unity of Being is discussed as a rule in works dealing with the Great Sheikh's treatment of *waḥdat al-wudjūd*.

4. See, e.g., T. Izutsu, *Sufism and Taoism*, p. 21; A. D. Knysh, *Mirovozzrenie Ibn ʿArabī. // Religii mira. Istoriya i soveremennost,' Yezhegodnik* (The Worldview of Ibn ʿArabī // In *Religions of the World: History and Modern Situation. An Annual*), Moscow, 1984, p. 86.

5. In Sufi poetry God and absolute beauty are frequently identified.

6. There are ninety-nine names of Allah mentioned in the Koran; Ibn ʿArabī speaks of "the infinite multitude" of Divine Names.

7. Compare Plotinus: Now it is clear that this one must be many, because it exists after the altogether One. . .there was also intellect, and life was in it; and perfect intellect and perfect life. Then it was not one as Intellect but all, and possessing all the particular intellects. . .and it was the "complete living being," not having only man in it; for otherwise there would only be man here below. . . .Well, the plants could fit into the argument; for the plant here is a rational forming principal resting life. . . For that first plant is certainly one, and these plants here are many, and necessarily come from one. If this is really so, that plant must be much more primarily alive and be this very thing, plant, and these here must live from it in the second and third degree and from its trees. . .If one enquires, therefore, where the living beings come from, one is enquiring where the sky there comes from; and this is to enquire where the [universal] living being comes from, and this is the same as where life comes from, and universal life and universal Soul and universal Intellect. . .They all flow, in a way, from a single spring. . .as if there was one quality which held and kept intact all the qualities in itself. . . . (*Plotinus*, Vol. 7, pp. 111–119).

8. This is an extract from the poem *Gulsan-i-rāz* (*The Secret Rose Garden*, composed by Maḥmūd ash-Shabistarī to answer eighteen questions put to him by a Sufi friend in 1311. A. Schimmel considers it "the handiest introduction to the thought of post-Ibn ʿArabī Sufism" (Mystical Dimensions, p. 280). It was so popular that in Iran it served

as a "traditional manual" of Sufism. It was—and surely not incidentally—one of the first Sufi books translated into European languages (in 1838 into German and in 1880 into English). This poem inspired M. Iqbal to create his *mathnawī, The New Rose Garden of Mystery* (published in 1927).

9. The orientalists hold different views on the pantheistic character of *waḥdat al-wujūd* and other trends in Sufism. Among those who apply that term to Sufism are A. von.-Kremer, I. Golgziher, R. A. Nicholson. Applying pantheism as a definition for any concept of Sufism has been strongly rejected by those who insist on the unacceptability of using non-Islamic notions to refer to Sufism (see S. H. Nasr, F. Schuon, M. A. Ling).

10. The most striking instance of naturalistic pantheism is presented by Giordano Bruno. See his thesis, "Natura . . . non e altro che Dio nelle cose" ("Nature is nothing else but God in things" [*Lo spaccio*, p. 154]).

11. See Naumkin's study preceding the Russian edition of the *Revival of Religious Sciences* (*Essays and Comments*, p. 22). This opinion is based mostly on information taken from the work of the medieval philosopher Moses Maimonides entitled *The Guide of the Perplexed*. The view was shared by Thomas Aquinas, Hegel, the prominent orientalists L. Massignon, H. Gibb, and many others, most modern Muslim authors included.

12. S. S. Averintsef has justly adverted to the extreme difficulty of distinguishing between pantheism and theism when the pantheist thesis "*anā 'l-Ḥaqq*" ("I am the Absolute Truth [God]) is to be compared with the theistic aphorism of the Koran (Sura 50, 15), according to which God is nearer to Man than his jugular artery (*Filosofskaya entsiklopedia*, 5:190).

13. T. K. Ibrahim discounts Maimonides' interpretation of *kalām*, considering it "tendentious" though he agrees that Mutazilites did assert creatio ex nihilo; Mutazilites-Jahmites rejected any approximation whatever between God and created things and thus came to allege the transcendence of God; Asharites maintained creatio ex nihilo. The main stimulus of Ibrahim's research consists in providing the *formality* of Mutakallims' theism and in making out that Asharites counterpoised immanent-transcendental pantheism to the spatiotemporal transcendentalism of Sunnism. It is hardly possible to accept this opinion if we consider the propositions of such prominent representatives of Asharism

as Abū Ḥāmid al-Ghazālī for example. Al-Ghazālī wrote in his *Revival of the Religious Sciences*: "There is only one Maker—the Almighty and. . .everything created—creatures and our daily bread, alms and abstinence—proceed from Him, life and death—were created and designed by Creator solely. . . .He is the unique and unprecedented Doer. Everything else acts by compulsion only and is unable to move by itself a simplest particle of the earthly or heavenly universe" (*Voskresenie*, p. 207).

14. A. V. Sagadeev has remarked that "of all the representatives of 'general public' the Sufi Gnostic came nearest to the philosophic ideals of Ibn Sīnā" (*Ibn-Sīnā*, p. 196).

Chapter Two. Anguish after the Hidden

1. R. A. Nicholson called Ibn 'Arabī "the father of Islamic pantheism" who constructed "the most imposing monument of mystical speculation the world has ever seen" (*Rūmī*, p. 24).

2. *Quṭb* ("the divine pole or axis") is a mystic who has attained perfection on the Path of realizing the Truth.

3. A mystic's exertions are directed at realization of the Truth as a certain superempirical eternal idea identical to Absolute Being, or God.

4. Compare Plato's treatment of the synthesis of love and perception as a sort of fury, an ecstasy (*Symposium* 203a–212a; *Phaedrus* 244a–257b).

5. It should be kept in mind that the term "apodictic" was introduced by Aristotle to denote scientific knowledge, absolutely true knowledge.

6. Compare also Fyodor Tyutchev's "Utter your thoughts. They flow in lies" (*Silentium*, p. 24).

7. Rūmī's 'Intellect' is similar to Plato's *nous*, elucidated as intellectual capacity directed at perceiving the notional content of things. This capacity distinguishes Man from animals and unites him with the Divine universe.

8. The 'niche' (*mishkāt*) is mentioned in the Koran (Sura 24, ayat 35):

> God is the Light
> Of the heavens and the earth.
> The parable of His Light

Is as if there were a Niche
And within it a Lamp:
The Lamp enclosed in Glass:
The Glass as it were
A brilliant star:
Lit from a blessed Tree,
An Olive, neither of the East
Nor of the West,
Whose Oil is well-nigh Luminous,
Though fire scarce touched it:
Light upon Light!
God doth guide
Whom He will
To His Light:
God doth set forth parables
For men: and God
Doth know all things.

9. "For once Christ died for our sins; and, rising from the dead, He dieth no more" (Augustine, *City of God*, p. 350).

10. The Koran says, "Of knowledge ye have been vouchsafed but little" (Sura 17; 85).

11. There are not a few examples in history of asserting the limitations of human knowledge being taken as premises of unbounded daring of human mind. K. E. Tsiolkovsky wrote, "All our knowledge, that of the past, of the present and of the future, is a thing of naught in comparison with what we shall never know."

Chapter Three. The Path of Perfection

1. Chuang-tzu is a prominent Tao thinker who lived in the late fourth century and the beginning of the third century B.C.

2. According to H. Abdalati, "The Quran has stated that truly God does not forgive the sin of shirk (polytheism, pantheism, trinity etc.)" (*Islam*, p. 33).

3. That was the comment on *dhikr* by Abū' l-Ḳāsim Ḳushayrī (d. ca. 1074).

4. See V. V. Naumkin's comments (*Essays*, p. 296).

5. The idea of fatalism is formulated by al-Ghazālī in his *Revival of the Religious Sciences*: "Everything between heaven and earth takes place according to the established regular order" (*Voskresenie*, p. 223).

6. Al-Ghazālī, again, saw very clearly that "To allow that all sins occur not by Allah's ordinance is impossible and it injures the belief in the One God. If all the sins come from the Almighty hate for them is hate for God's ordaining. How can such opposites be combined and how can love and hate be joined together?" (Voskresenie, p. 255).

7. Koranic interpretation asserts that good comes from God and evil from Man: "Whatever of good befalleth thee (O man) it is from Allah, and whatever of ill befalleth thee it is from thyself" (Sura 4; 79).

8. In Islamic mythology Iblīs presumed he was superior to Man because he had been born of fire and Man had been made from dust and clay.

9. The subject of birds' converse (an allogoric description of the mystical path) is quite well represented in Arabian and Persian literature. There is Ibn Sīnā's *Risālat aṭ-ṭair* (*Treatise about Birds*) and al-Ghazālī's story with the same title recounting birds' pilgrimage. It is supposed that this conceit was founded upon mention of birds in the Koran:

> Behold! Abraham said:
> My Lord! Show me how
> Thou givest life to the dead."
> He said: "Dost thou not
> Then believe?" He said:
> "Yea! but to satisfy
> My own understanding."
> He said: "Take four birds;
> Take them to turn to thee;
> Put a portion of them
> On every hill, and call to them:
> They will come to thee
> (Flying) with speed.
> Then know that God
> Is Exalted in Power, Wise. (Sura 2; 260)

The commentators of the Koran associate the four birds with a peacock, a duck, a crow, and a cock that symbolize, respectively, mundane adornments, greed, insatiability, and lust. Thus the sacred book is envisaged to teach a lesson: "Turn your eyes away from the adornments of this world and from taking a pride in them, and from covetousness in searching for your share, and from appeasing your lust, that you may achieve true perfection in your faith. And when you have set your soul free from those proclivities, you will embellish it with my attribute on the day when the dead are resurrected" Ye. E. Bertels, (*Sufism*, p. 76).

10. *Tē* is Tao revealed in things and men; it is a manifestation of Tao potencies in the phenomenal world. It may be translated as Virtue.

11. This refers to the custom of making pilgrimage to the tombs of saints (*walī*).

Chapter Four. Sufism and Modernity

1. Engels drew attention to the fact that revolutionary opposition to fuedalism often took the shape of mysticism. "It is well-known how much sixteenth-century reformers depended on mysticism. Munzer himself was indebted to it" (*The Peasant War in Germany* // Karl Marx and Friedrich Engels. *Collected Works*. Moscow, 1978, 10:413).

2. "The spirit" of Rūmī is present, for example, in a poem in memory of Nazim Hikmet written by Iraq poet Abdal Vahab al-Bayati. Ali Shariati (d. 1978) conjures up Rūmī when speaking about the modern degradation of Muslim society, about the necessity of national and religious revival ("Art Awaiting," p. 7).

3. The mystical behest "Renounce yourself" was metamorphosed into the formula of highest civil morals. Aleksandr Blok wrote: "This formula is repeated effectually by *every* man; he cannot help running against it invariably if his spiritual life is tolerably strenuous. . . . I am sure, it contains the cure for the disease of 'irony', which is the disease of a personal self, the disease of 'individualism' " (*Ironia*, 5:349).

4. Marx appraised European romanticism as "Die erste Reaktion gegen die franzosische Revolution" ("the first reaction against the French revolution" of 1789 [*Letter*, Bd. 32, S. 51]).

5. Gibran was educated (in a lay institution) in Beirut, then in a Paris school of fine arts, and then in the United States. In the United States he headed a group of Arab emigrant writers, "The Pen League."

6. A collection of Gibran's essays and stories was entitled "The Storms," and M. Na'īmā's article about him bore the title "Storms of 'The Storms.' "

Select Bibliography

Abdalati, H. *Islam in Focus*. Indianapolis, 1977.

Adams, Ch. *Islam and Modernism in Egypt*. London, 1933.

Affifi, A. E. *The Muslim Philosophy of Ibnu' l-'Arabī*. Cambridge, 1938.

Anawati, G. C., and L. Gardet. *Mystique musulmane: aspects et tendences, expèriences et techniques*. P., 1976.

Amīr, Khusrau. *Diwan-ikamil*, ed. Mahmud Darwish. Tehran, 1964 (in Persian).

———. *Memorial Volume*. New Delhi, 1975

Ibn 'Arabī. *Fuṣūṣ al-ḥikam*. Beirut, 1980 (in Arabic).

———. *The Wisdom of the Prophets*. Alsworth, Gloucestershire, 1975

———. *Les illuminations de la Mecque. The Meccan Illuminations: Selected Texts*. Sous la direction de Chodkiewicz M., P., 1988.

Arberry, A. J. *Classical Persian Literature*. L., 1958.

———. *Sufism: An Account of the Mystics of Islam*. New York and Evanston, 1970.

'Aṭṭār, Farīduddīn. *Manṭiq aṭ-ṭayr*, ed. Jawad Shakur. Tehran, 1962.

Austin, R. W. J. Introduction//*Sufis of Andalusia: The Rūh al-quds and al-durrat al-fākhīrah of Ibn 'Arabī*. Translated with introduction and notes by R. W. J. Austin. Berkeley-Los Angeles, 1977.

Augustine. *The City of God*. Translated by Marius Dodd. Chicago, 1977.

Averintsev, S. S. Theism. Sofia.//*Filosofskaya entsiklopedia* (The Encyclopaedia of Philosophy). Vol. 5. Moscow, 1970.

Averroes (Ibn Rushd). *Tahafut al-Tahafut* (The Incoherence of the Incoherence). Translated by Simon Van den Bergh. London, 1954.

Bakhtin, M. M. *Problemy poetiki Dostoevskogo* (The Problems of Dostoyevsky's Poetics). Moscow, 1979.

Bertels, Ye. E. *Sufism i sufiyskaya literatura.//Izbrannye trudy,* III (Sufism and Sufi Literature.//Selected Works, vol. 3). Moscow, 1965.
The Bhagavadgītā or The Song Divine. Gorakhpur, 1958.
Blok, Aleksandr. *Ironia* (The Irony).// *Sobranie sochineniy,* V (Collected Works, vol. 5). Moscow-Leningrad, 1962.
Brown, E. G. *Literary History of Persia.* Vols. 1–4. London, 1902.
Bruno, Giordano. *Lo spaccio della bestia trionfante.* Milano, 1970.
Chittick, W. C. *The Sufi Path of Love: The Spiritual Teachings of Rumi.* Albany, 1983.
———. *The Sufi Path of Knowledge: Ibn al-ʿArabī's Metaphysics of Imagination.* Albany 1989.
———. *Faith and Practice of Islam.* Albany, 1992.
Chuang-tzu. *The Complete Works.* New York-London, 1968.
Collected Papers on Islamic Philosophy and Mysticism. Tehran, 1971.
Corbin, H. *Creative Imagination in the Sufism of Ibn ʿArabī.* Princeton, 1969.
Dante, Aligheri. *La Divina Commedia*, Milano, 1899.
———. *The Divine Comedy.* Translated by N. W. Longfellow. Boston-New York, 1895
Dehlevi, Hosrov. *Izbrannoye.* (Selected Works). Tashkent, 1980.
Eckart, Johannes (Meister Eckhart). *On the Divine Birth in the Soul.*//Happold, F. C. *Mysticism: A Study and an Anthology.* Middlesex-Baltimore, 1973.
Emre, Yūnus. *Divan.*//Schimmel, A. M. *Mystical Dimensions of Islam.* Chapel Hill, 1978.
Encyclopaedia of Islam. 4 vols. Leiden, 1954–80.
Enclclopaedia of Philosophy. 8 vols. New York-London, 1972.
Encyclopaedia of Religion and Ethics, Vol. 12. Edinburgh-New York, 1954.
Engels, F. *Bruno Bauer and Early Christianity,* Karl Marx and Friedrich Engels. *Collected Works.* Vol. 24. New York, 1989.
———. *Letters*//Karl Marx and Friedrich Engels, *Collected Works.* Vol. 2. Moscow, 1975.
Al-Fārābī. *Filosofskie tractaty* (Philosophical Treatises). Alma-Ata, 1970.
Ibn al-Fāriḍ, Umar. *Tā'iyyat al-kubrā.* //Nicholson, R. A. *Studies in Islamic Mysticism.* Delhi, 1981.
Frank, S. L. *Sochineniya.* (Writings) Moscow, 1990.
Friedmann, Y. *Shaykh Aḥmad Sirhindī: An Outline of His Thought and a Study of His Image in the Eyes of Posterity.* Montreal-London, 1971.

Frolova, Ye. A. *Problema very i znannia v arabskoy filosofii*. (The Problem of Faith and Knowledge in the Arabian Philosophy). Moscow, 1983.

Ghalib, Mirza Asadulla. *Dīwān*.//*Interpretations of Ghalib* by J. L. Kaul. Delhi, 1957.

Al-Ghazālī, Abū Ḥāmid. *Voskresenie nauk o vere* (The Revival of Religious Sciences. Translated by V. V. Naumkin with his introduction and comments). Moscow, 1980.

Gibran, Khalil. *The Prophet*. New York, 1934.

Goldziher,I. *Die Islamische Philosophie*//Allgemeine Geschichte der Philosophie von Wilhelm Wundt, H. Oldenberg, Ignaz Goldziher, Wilhelm Grabe, T. Inouge, H. von Arnim, Clemens Baumker, W. Windelband. Berlin-Leipzig, 1909.

———. *Introduction to Islamic Theology and Law*. Translated by A. and R. Hamori. Princeton, 1981.

A. Ya. Gurevich *Categorii srednevekovoi cultury* (Categories of the Medieval Culture). Moscow, 1984.

Ḥāfiẓ of Shiraz. *Selections from his Poems*. Translated by H. Bicknell. London, 1875.

Al-Ḥallāj, Ḥusayn ibn Manṣūr. *Divān*.//Journal Asiatique. Paris, Janvier-Juillet, 1931.

———. *Kitab aṭ-ṭawāsīn*.//Massignon, L. La Passion d'al-Ḥosayn ibn Mansour al-Hallāj, martyr mystique de l'Islam. Paris, 1922.

Happold, F. C. *Mysticism: A Study and an Anthology*. Harmondsworth, Middlesex, and Baltimore, 1973.

Hegel, G. W. F. *Werke*. Berlin, 1840–45 (Zweite Auflage).

———. *Lectures on the History of Philosophy*. 3 vols. Translated by S. Haldane. London, 1892–96. Reprint 1955.

———. *Lectures on the Philosophy of the World History*. Translated by H. B. Nisbet. Cambridge-London, 1975.

———. *Hegel's Logic*. Translated by W. Wallace. London, 1931.

———. *Hegel's Philosophy of Mind*. Translated by W. Wallace. Oxford, 1894.

A History of Muslim Philosophy. 2 vols. Wiesbaden, 1963–66.

Ibrahim, T. K. *Philosofia kalama* (The Philosophy of Kalam). Moscow, 1984.

Iqbal, A. *The Impact of Mawlana Jalaluddin Rūmī on Islamic Culture*. Tehran, 1974.

Iqbal, Muhammad. *The Reconstruction of Religious Thought in Islam*. Lahore, 1962.

———. *Payūm-i-mashriq*. Lahore, 1958.

———. Kiernan, V. G. *Poems from Iqbal*. London, 1955.

———. *A Message from the East*. Translation by M. Hadi Hussain, Karachi, 1971.

Krimsky, R. *Istoriya Persii, eye literatura i teosophiya derveshisma*. (History of Persia. Its Literature and Dervish Theosophy,) Moscow, 1914–17.

Izutsu, Toshihiko. *Sufism and Taoism: A Comparative Study of Key Philosophical Concepts*. Berkeley-Los Angeles-London, 1983.

Jāmī, Maulānā 'Abdurraḥmān. *Diwān-i kāmil*. Ed. Hāshim Rizā. Tehran, 1341 sh./1962.

Jīlī, 'Abdul-Karīm al-. *Al-insān al-kāmil*.//Nicholson, R. A., *Studies in Islamic Mysticism*. Delhi, 1981.

Hromova, K. A., and V. G. Malushkov. *Poiski putei reformatsii v islame: opit irana* (The Search of the Ways to Reformation in Islam: An Iranian Experience). Moscow, 1991.

Lahbabi, M. S. *Le personnalisme musulman*. Paris, 1964.

Lenin V. S. *The Attitude of the Workers' Party to Religion.//Collected Works* Vol. 15. Moscow, 1963

Lenin, V. S. *Socialism and Religion//Collected Works*. vol. 10. Moscow, 1962.

Ling, T. O. *Islam's Alternative to Fundamentalism*. Manchester, 1981.

Lings, M. *Sufi Saint of the Twentieth Century*. London, 1972.

———. *What Is Sufism*? London, 1975.

Maimonides, Moses. *The Guide for the Perplexed*. 3 vols. New York, 1946.

Marx, Karl. *Contribution to the Critique to Hegel's Philosophy of Law. Introduction*.//Karl Marx and Friedrich Engels. *Collected Works*. Vol. 3. Moscow, 1975.

Marx, Karl. *A Letter to F. Engels, March 25, 1868.* //Karl Marx and Friedrich Engels. *Werke*. Bd. 32, Berlin, 1965.

———. *The War Question*.//Karl Marx and Friedrich Engels. *Collected Works*. Vol. 12. Moscow, 1979.

Marx, Karl, and Friedrich Engels. *The German Ideology*.//Karl Marx and Friedrich Engels. *Collected Works*. Vol. 5. Moscow, 1976.

Massignon, Louis. *La passion d'al*-Ḥosayn ibn Mansour al-Ḥallāj, martyr mystique de l'Islam, ex*écuté à Bagdad le 26 mars 922*. 2 vols. Paris, 1922.

———. Tasawwuf.//*Encyclopaedia of Islam*. Vol. 4. Leiden, 1980.

Nag-Hammadi Codices. Leiden, 1975. See also Trofimova, M. K. *Istoriko-filosofskie voprosy gnosticisma* (Historico-Philosophic Problems of Gnosticism). Moscow, 1979.

Nasr S. H. *The Encounter of Man and Nature: The Spiritual Crisis of Modern Man*. London, 1968.

———. *Ideals and Realities of Islam*. London, 1966.

———. *An Introduction to Islamic Cosmological Doctrines*. Cambridge, Mass., 1964.

———. *Islamic Life and Thought*. 1981.

———. *Islamic Studies—Essays on Law and Society, the Science, Philosophy and Sufism*. Beirut, 1967.

———. *Knowledge and the Sacred*. Edinburgh, 1981.

———. *Science and Civilization in Islam*. Cambridge, Mass., 1968.

———. *Sufi Essays*. New York, 1977.

———. *Three Muslim Sages: Avicenna—Suhravardi—Ibn ʿArabī*. Cambridge, Mass., 1964.

———. *The Western World and Its Challenges to Islam.//Islamic Quarterly*. Vol. 17. London, 1973.

Naumkin, V. V. *Essays and Comments on al-Ghazālī's "Revival of the Religious Sciences*."//Abū Ḥāmid al-Ghazālī. *Voskresenie nauk o vere*. Moscow, 1980.

Nicholson, R. A. *Rumi: Poet and Mystic*. London, 1950.

———. *Selected Poems from the Divani Shamsi Tabriz*. Cambridge, 1961.

———. *Studies in Islamic Mysticism*. Delhi, 1981.

———. Sufis.//*Encyclopaedia of Religion and Ethics*. Vol. 12. Edinburgh-New York, 1954.

Plotinus. Translated by A. M. Armstrong, Vol. 7, Cambridge, London, 1988.

Poincaré, Henri. *Mathematical Creation*.//Hadamard, J. *An Essay on the Psychology of Invention in the Mathematical Field*. Princeton, 1945.

Prigarina, N. I. *Poetika tvorchestva Muhammada Iqbala* (The Poetics of Muhammad Iqbal's Creative Work). Moscow, 1978.

Prozorov, S. M. Vvedenie (Introductory essay).//*Ash-Shahrastani. Kniga o religiyakh i sectakh* (ash-Shahrastani. The Book of Sects and Creeds). Moscow, 1984.

Rahman, F. *Islam*. London, 1966.

Renan, Ernest. *Averroès et l'averroisme*. Paris, 1882.

Rosenthal, Franz. *Knowledge Triumphant: The Concept of Knowledge in Medieval Islam*. Leiden, 1970.

The Rubaiyat of Sarmad. Introduction and translation by Abul Kalam Azad. New Delhi, 1991.

Rūmī, al-Balkhī Maulānā Jalāluddīn. *Discourses of Rumi*. Translated, introduction, and notes by A. J. Arberry. New York, 1977.

———. *Dīwān*.//Nicholson, R. A. *Selected Poems from the "Divan-i Shams-i Tabriz*. Cambridge, 1961.

———. *The Mathnawī*. Translated and commentary by R. A. Nicholson. 8 vols. London, 1925–40.

———. *The Spiritual Couplets*. Translated and abridged by E. H. Whinfield. London, 1898.

Ibn-Rushd (*Averroes*). *On the harmony of Religion and Philosophy*. London, 1961.

Sagadeev, A. V. *Ibn-Rushd*. Moscow, 1973

———. *Ibn-Sina*. Moscow, 1980.

Shimmel, Annemarie. *Mystical Dimensions of Islam*. Chapel Hill, 1978.

———. *Pain and Grace: A Study of Two Mystical Writers of Eighteenth Century Muslim India*. Leiden, 1976.

———. *The Triumphal Sun: A Study of the Works of Jalāloddin Rumi*. London and the Hague, 1978.

Schuon, Frithjof. *Understanding Islam*. London, 1976.

Shabistarī, Maḥmūd. *Gulhsan-i rāz*: The Rose-Garden of Mysteries. Edited and translated by E. H. Whinfield. London, 1880.

Shah Idries. *The Way of the Sufi*. Markham (Canada), 1974.

Shariati, Ali. Art Awaiting the Saviour?//*News and Views*. Vol. 1, no. 132.

A Shorter Encyclopaedia of Islam. Leiden-London, 1971.

Inb-Sīnā. *Avicenna on Theology*. Translated by A. J. Arberry. London, 1951.

Smirnov, A. V. *Filosofia Ibn Arabi* (Philosophy of Ibn ʿArabī). Ph.D. Thesis, Moscow, 1989.

Smith, M. *Studies in Early Mysticism in the Near and Middle East*. Amsterdam, 1973.

Sufism v kontekste musulmanskoi kulture (Sufism in the Context of the Muslim Culture). Moscow, 1989.

Trimingham, J. S. *The Sufi Orders in Islam*. London-Oxford-New York, 1973.

Trofimova, M. K. *Istoriko-filosofscie voprosy gnostitsisma* (Histotico-Philosophic Problems of Gnosticism). Moscow, 1979.

Tyutchev, Fyodor. *Silentium*.//*Three Russian Poets: Selections from Pushkin, Lermontov, and Tyutchev*, Norfolk, 1944.

Vahid, S. A. *Thoughts and Reflections of Iqbal*. Lahore, 1964.
Vahiduddin, S. *Islam in India: Studies and Commentaries*. Vol. 3. *Islamic Experience in Contemporary Thought*. Delhi, 1986.
Waley, A. *The Way and Its Power: A Study of the Tao Tẹ̌ Ching*. London, 1956.

Index